I0488093

These Human Rights Agents Lied through Their Teeth!

Why is That?

No Reply Yet!

Index **Page**

Chapter 1

I don't expect much from you, but nevertheless this is my complaint!

July 10, 2014

Jennifer Stoddart, Privacy Commissioner
Place de Ville, Tower B
112 Kent St, 3rd Flr
Ottawa, ON K1A 1H3

Of the 400 + pages on this disk received from David Langtry, Chief Commissioner, Canadian Human Rights Commission – over ½ are blank!!

There is no information whatsoever about processing my complaint due to:

Access to all information related to the acceptance and processing of Mental PTSD Discrimination Complaint dated May 21, 2014, Employment from 1976 to the present, based on lies perpetrated by CHRC agents Lorisa Stein and Nicole Bomberg, and most recently by Marie Josee Frenette who said I have never made a complaint against the RCMP?

I don't expect much from you, but nevertheless this is my complaint.

Mr.X. , BA, BSW, MA
former federal peace officer,
PTSD Disability Pensioner,
Old Age Pensioner

ALWAYS HOME – HOWEVER, SOMEONE IS SCREWING WITH MY PHONE – IS I THE SAME ONES THAT AR TRYING TO SHOVE A VIRUS IN MY COMPUTER OR COMPLAINING ABOUT THIS??

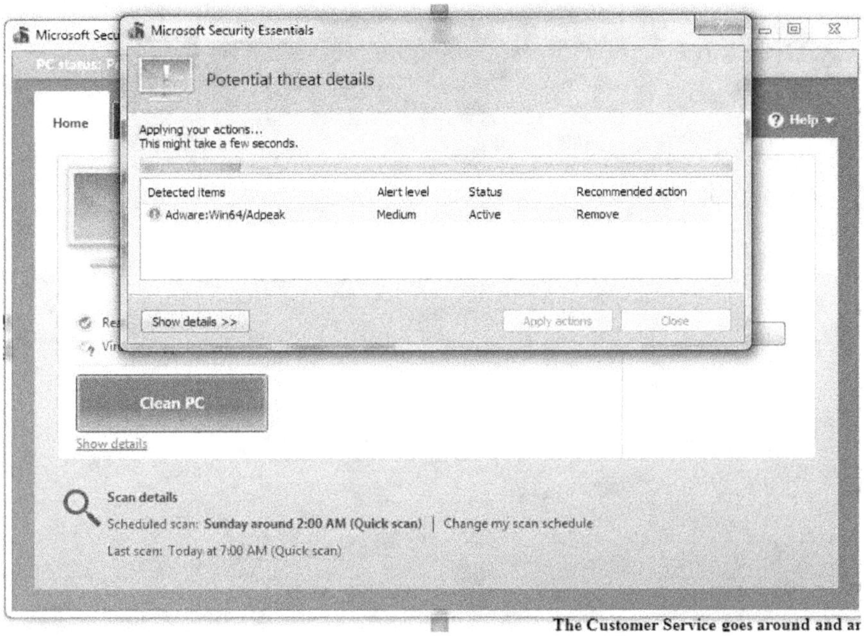

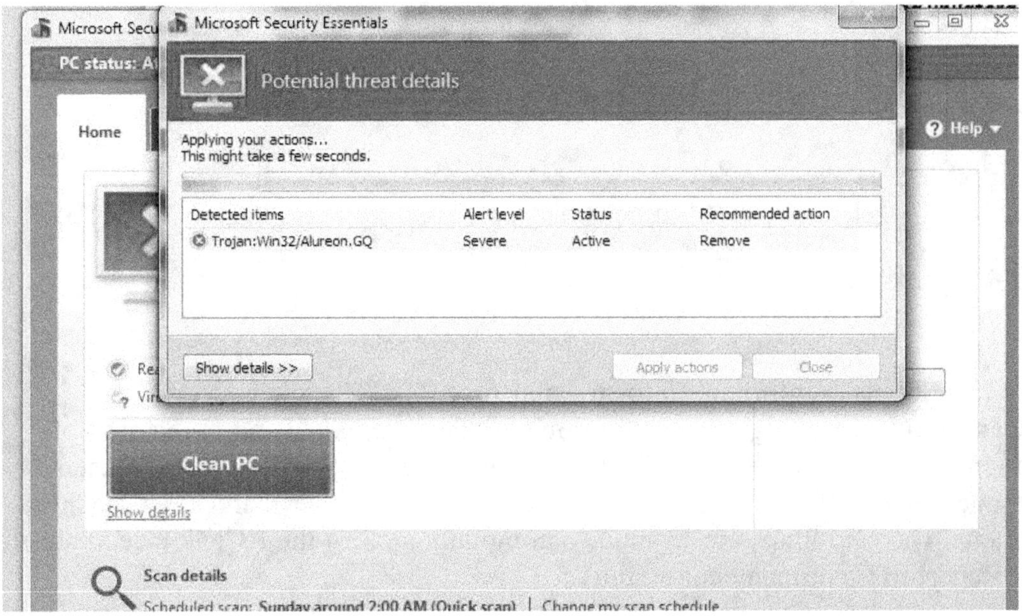

Chapter 2

Canadian Human Rights Commission agents Lorisa Stein, Nicole Bomberg and Marie Josee Frenette Lie through Their Teeth!

June 22, 2014

Access to Information and Privacy Division
Canadian Human Rights Commission
344 Slater Street
Ottawa, Ontario K1A 1E1
ATIP.AIPRP@CHRC-CCDP.GC.CA

David Langtry
Chief Commissioner
Canadian Human Rights Commission
344 Slater Street, 8th Floor
Ottawa, Ontario K1A 1E1
Toll Free: 1-888-214-1090
Fax: 613-996-9661
registrar@chrt-tcdp.gc.ca
communications@chrc-ccdp.gc.ca
library@chrc-ccdp.ca

Access to all information related to the acceptance and processing of Mental PTSD Discrimination Complaint dated May 21, 2014, Employment from 1976 to the present, based on lies perpetrated by CHRC agents Lorisa Stein and Nicole Bomberg, and most recently by Marie Josee Frenette who said I have never made a complaint against the RCMP [see attached Access Request & Book Report to accompany Access Request].

Retaliation against Mr.X. by Canadian Human Rights Commission for making an initial complaint about Mental PTSD Disability Employment Discrimination against RCMP as federal peace officer at the time, where CHRC agents Lorisa Stein and Nicole Bomberg lied so as to not process Mr.X. 's legitimate CHRC complaint!!

Please find attached my Access to information form dated June 22, 2014 related to the disposition of the Canadian Human Rights Commission a to the acceptance and processing of Mental Discrimination Complaint dated May 21, 2014, Employment from 1976 to the present, based on lies perpetrated by CHRC agents Lorisa Stein and Nicole Bomberg, and most recently by Marie Josee Frenette who said I have never made a complaint against the RCMP [see attached Complaint & Book Report to accompany complaint].

Retaliation against Mr.X. by Canadian Human Rights Commission for making an initial complaint about Mental Disability Employment Discrimination against RCMP as federal peace officer at the time, where CHRC agents Lorisa Stein and Nicole Bomberg lied so as to not process Mr.X. 's legitimate CHRC complaint!!

Thank you,

Mr.X. , BA, BSW, MA
former federal peace officer,
PTSD Disability Pensioner,
Old Age Pensioner

cc. Peter Gordon MacKay, MP
Attorney General
219 Main Street, No 303
Antigonish, Nova Scotia B2G 2C1
peter.mackay@parl.gc.ca
peter.mackay.C1@parl.gc.ca

cc. Paul Crampton
Chief Justice
Federal Court, Ottawa, Ontario K1A 0H9
media-fct@fct-cf.gc.ca

Beverley McLachlin, P.C.,
Chief Justice of Canada
Supreme Court of Canada
301 Wellington Street, Ottawa, Ontario K1A 0J1
media@scc-csc.ca

Government of Canada / Gouvernement du Canada

Info Source

Privacy Act

Personal Information Request Form

Protected when completed

For official use only

Step 1
Determine which federal government institution is most likely to hold personal information about you. Decide whether you wish to submit an informal request for the information or a formal request under the *Privacy Act*. If you wish to make an informal request, contact the appropriate institution. The address can likely be found in ***Info Source*** publications which are available across Canada, generally in major public and academic libraries, constituency offices of federal Members of Parliament and most federal government public enquiry and service offices.

Step 2
To apply for personal information about you under the *Privacy Act*, complete this form. Describe the information being sought and provide any relevant details necessary to help the institution find it. If you require assistance, refer to ***Info Source (Sources of Federal Government Information)*** for a description of personal information banks held by the institution or contact its Privacy Coordinator.

Step 3
Forward the personal information request form to the Privacy Coordinator of the institution holding the information. The address is listed in the "Introduction" to ***Info Source***.

Step 4
When you receive an answer to your request, review the information to determine whether you wish to make a further request under the Act. You also have the right to complain to the Privacy Commissioner should you believe that you have been denied any of your rights under the Act.

Federal Government Institution Canadian Human Rights Commission

I wish to examine the information ☐ As it is ☒ All in English ☐ All in French

Provide details regarding the information being sought

Access to all information related to the acceptance and processing of Mental Discrimination Complaint dated May 21, 2014, Employment from 1976 to the present, based on lies perpetrated by CHRC agents Lorisa Stein and Nicole Bomberg, and most recently by Marie Josee Frenette who said I have never made a complaint against the RCMP – IN Retaliation for making complaint against RCMP [see attached Complaint & Book Report to accompany complaint].

Method of access preferred ☒ Receive copies of originals ☐ Examine originals in government offices

Name of applicant BA, BSW, MA

Street

Prov

I request access to personal information about myself under the Privacy Act as I am a Canadian citizen, permanent resident or another individual, including an i

June 22, 2014
Date

Chapter 3

Retaliation against Mr.X. by Canadian Human Rights Commission for making an initial complaint about Mental Disability Employment Discrimination!

21 May, 2014

David Langtry
Acting Chief Commissioner
Canadian Human Rights Commission
344 Slater Street, 8th Floor
Ottawa, Ontario K1A 1E1
Toll Free: 1-888-214-1090
Fax: 613-996-9661
registrar@chrt-tcdp.gc.ca

Marie Josee Frenette, Agent
Canadian Human Rights Commission
344 Slater Street, 8th Floor
Ottawa, Ontario K1A 1E1
communications@chrc-ccdp.gc.ca
library@chrc-ccdp.ca

RE: Marie Josee Frenette, CHRC Agent – You lied in your correspondence to me dated 12 May, 2014

You lied in your correspondence to me dated 12 May, 2014 when you said I had never made a Canadian Human Rights Commission complaint.

My initial complaint was based on my mental disability of PTSD – Chronic Type was caused by RCMP illegal acts as per Federal Court Action T-1131-83 and as complained to the Canadian Human Rights Commission in the initial complaint.

My complaint was based on Employment Discrimination with the Canadian Penitentiary Service due to my mental disability of PTSD – Chronic Type was caused by RCMP illegal acts as per Federal Court Action T-1131-83 and as complained to the Canadian Human Rights Commission in the initial complaint.

You have access to Federal Court Action T-1131-83 and you have access to my initial complaint in which Canadian Human Rights Commission agents Nicole Bomberg and Lorisa Stein lied so as to not look or process my initial Canadian Human Rights Commission complaint!

RE: Retaliation for making an initial complaint to the CHRC, and this current Complaint against the Canadian Human Rights Commission for Retaliation for making the first complaint – A Discrimination Violation under your own Act:

☑ Retaliation for having filed a previous complaint under the Canadian Human Rights Act

As cited 2012-10-16 (Docket: T1340/7008) in First Nations Child and Family Caring Society of Canada et al. v. Attorney General of Canada (for the Minister of Indian and Northern Affairs Canada), 2012 CHRT 24 (CanLII), the court held:

The Complainants' allegations of retaliation emanate from the same factual matrix as the initial complaint as both complaints share the same Complainants and the retaliatory events alleged are linked to the filing of the initial complaint against the Respondent.

In other words, my current complaint cannot be separated from the initial Canadian Human Rights Commission complaint, for Retaliation for making the first complaint – otherwise the Canadian Human Rights Commission would be thwarting the fair administration of justice and hinder the panel's ability to conduct the proceedings in the most informal and expeditious manner, as the requirements of natural justice and rules of procedure allow as mandated by paragraph 48.9(1) of the Act.

RE: Diability Discrimination because CHRC would have to include evidence that my mental disability of PTSD – Chronic Type was caused by RCMP illegal acts as per Federal Court Action T-1131-83 and as complained to the Canadian Human Rights Commission in the initial complaint where Canadian Human Rights Commission agents Nicole Bomberg and Lorisa Stein lied so as to not look or process my initial Canadian Human Rights Commission complaint:

As further cited on 2008-10-03 in Dawson v. Canada Post Corporation, 2008 CHRT 41 (CanLII),this court held it is the mandate of the Canadian Human Rights Commission to:

"get rid of any discriminatory behavior in the workplace as well as in society in general. It is worth reminding employers as well as society as a whole that the purpose of the Canadian Human Rights Act, as stated in section 2 of the Act, is to give effect to the principle that all individuals should have an opportunity equal with other individuals to make for themselves the lives that they are able and wish to have and to have their needs accommodated, consistent with their duties and obligations as members of society, without being hindered in or prevented from doing so by discriminatory practices based on race, national or ethnic origin, colour, religion, age, sex, sexual orientation, marital status, family status, disability or conviction for an offence for which a pardon has been granted."

In my initial complaint Canadian Human Rights Commission agents Nicole Bomberg and Lorisa Stein lied so as to not look or process my initial Canadian Human Rights Commission complaint because my mental disability of PTSD – Chronic Type was caused by RCMP illegal acts as per Federal Court Action T-1131-83 and as complained to the Canadian Human Rights Commission in the initial complaint!

Hence, the Canadian Human Rights Commission by Nicole Bomberg's and Lorisa Stein's in their memos of my initial Canadian Human Rights Commission, the actions of Nicole Bomberg and Lorisa Stein has thwarted a conclusion to my initial Canadian Human Rights Commission complaint.

Likewise, the current lies by Marie Josee Frenette, CHRC Agent in her lettered dated 12 May, 2014 is a current effort to thwart my complaint of retaliation by the Canadian Human Rights Commission for making an initial complaint based on Employment Discrimination with the Canadian Penitentiary Service due to my mental disability of PTSD – Chronic Type was caused by RCMP illegal acts as per Federal Court Action T-1131-83 and as complained to the Canadian Human Rights Commission in the initial complaint.

RE: Canadian Human Rights Commission Agents Lorisa Stein and Nicole Bomberg lied in initial CHRC complaint, so no investigation was conducted of Discrimination Complaint to help protect the RCMP from embarrassment or court action / reprimand:

As also cited 2009-02-11 (Docket: A-360-08), in Leung v. Canada (Revenue Agency), 2009 FCA 38 (CanLII), the court held:

"Thus, in my view, the investigator failed to properly investigate an issue that goes to the essence of the complaint, in that she failed to make a proper inquiry into the classification process which resulted in the appellant having to compete for the new position. It is difficult to understand why the record remains obscure on this matter, considering that the information required to clarify the matter should be readily available from the employer."

In my initial complaint to the Canadian Human Rights Commission, CHRC Agents Lorisa Stein and Nicole Bomberg purposefully lied in initial CHRC complaint, so no investigation was conducted of Discrimination Complaint to help protect the RCMP from embarrassment or court action / reprimand!

Likewise, the current lies by Marie Josee Frenette, CHRC Agent in her lettered dated 12 May, 2014 is a current effort to thwart my complaint of retaliation by the Canadian Human Rights Commission for making an initial complaint based on Employment Discrimination with the Canadian Penitentiary Service due to my mental disability of PTSD – Chronic Type was caused by RCMP illegal acts as per Federal Court Action T-1131-83 and as complained to the Canadian Human Rights Commission in the initial complaint.

In conclusion Marie Josee Frenette, Canadian Human Rights Commission Agent, you purposefully lied in your correspondence to me date 12 May, 2014 where you lied and said I had never made a CHRC complaint before!

The nice thing about LIARS, such as yourself, liars always include something in the documents they send me – just as I received a copy of RCMP S/Sgt John Thomas Randle's 1979 letter with its lies in it, that formed the successful Federal Court Action T-1131-83 in my previous access request.

Likewise, in my previous access request, I was also sent the 1979 memos by Canadian Human Rights Commission LIARS Nicole Bomberg and Loisa Stein that also formed part of the successful Federal Court Action T-1131-83.

And now we come to another Canadian Human Rights Commission LIAR - Marie Josee Frenette, CHRC Agent, who also purposefully lied in her correspondence to me date 12 May, 2014 where she lied and said I had never made a CHRC complaint before!

Mr.X. , BA, BSW, MA
former federal peace officer
PTSD Disability Pensioner
Old Age Pensioner

cc. Paul Crampton
Chief Justice
Federal Court
Ottawa, Ontario
Canada K1A 0H9
media-fct@fct-cf.gc.ca

Beverley McLachlin, P.C.,
Chief Justice of Canada
Supreme Court of Canada
301 Wellington Street
Ottawa, Ontario K1A 0J1
media@scc-csc.ca

Jean Crowder, NDP
Consultant, human resources consultant, manager
jean.crowder@parl.gc.ca,

Carolyn Bennett, Liberal
Physician
carolyn.bennett@parl.gc.ca,

Craig Scott, NDP
No military service has been indexed for this parliamentarian
craig.scott@parl.gc.ca

Scott Simms, Liberal
Broadcaster, Journalist
scott.simms@parl.gc.ca

Randall Garrison, NDP
Criminal justice instructor, city councillor
randall.garrison@parl.gc.ca

Wayne Marston, NDP
Recipient of the Medal of Bravery in 1987
wayne.marston@parl.gc.ca

Irwin Cotler, Liberal
Lawyer, professor of law
irwin.cotler@parl.gc.ca

Irene Mathyssen, NDP
Community activist, teacher
irene.mathyssen@parl.gc.ca

John McCallum, Liberal
Author, economist, professor
john.mccallum@parl.gc.ca

Justin Trudeau, Liberal
No military service has been indexed for this parliamentarian
justin.trudeau@parl.gc.ca

Niki Ashton, NDP
Instructor, lecturer, researcher
niki.ashton@parl.gc.ca

Kirsty Duncan, Liberal
Athlete, author, geographer, lecturer, professor
kirsty.duncan@parl.gc.ca

Thomas Mulcair, NDP
Lawyer, professor
thomas.mulcair@parl.gc.ca

Elizabeth May, Green Party
Activist, environmentalist, executive director, lawyer, writer
elizabeth.may@parl.gc.ca

Did David Langtry, Canadian Human Rights Commissioner, infect my computer in retaliation for complaint about CHRC liars, in their attempts to stifle my complaint about Mental Disability [caused by RCMP illegal acts] Employment Discrimination!!!

Detected item	Alert level	Date
VirTool:Win32/CeeInject.gen!KK	Severe	24/05/2014 10:36 AM

VirTool:Win32/CeeInject.gen!KK

This is a generic detection for malicious files that are hidden, or obfuscated, to protect them from detection and analysis.

Detected item	Alert level	Date
Trojan:Win32/Alureon.GQ	Severe	24/05/2014 6:42 AM

Trojan:Win32/Alureon.GQ

Trojan:Win32/Alureon.GQ is a member of the Win32/Alureon family of malware - a family of data-stealing malware. These trojans allow an attacker to intercept incoming and outgoing Internet traffic in order to gather confidential information from your computer, such as user names, passwords, and credit card data.

The trojan is also used to generate traffic to specific URLs.

Win32/Alureon can also allow an attacker to transmit malicious data to your computer. It might modify DNS settings on your computer to enable the attacker to perform these tasks.

Detected item	Alert level	Date
Trojan:Win32/Alureon.GQ	Severe	24/05/2014 6:41 AM
TrojanDownloader:Win32/Zemot	Severe	24/05/2014 6:41 AM

TrojanDownloader:Win32/Zemot

This threat can download other malware onto your PC.

Detected item	Alert level	Date
Trojan:Win32/Alureon.GQ	Severe	24/05/2014 6:03 AM
PWS:Win32/Zbot.gen!AP	Severe	23/05/2014 10:07 PM
Trojan:Win32/Tesch	Severe	21/05/2014 1:50 PM
TrojanDropper:Win32/Vawtrak.A	Severe	21/05/2014 1:50 PM

Trojan.Win32.Tesch

Trojan:Win32/Tesch is a Trojan that targets the Windows platform. This malware communicates with a remote server and receives instructions from an attacker.

TrojanDropper:Win32/Vawtrak.A

This threat is classified as a trojan dropper. As its name suggests, a dropper trojan contains malicious or potentially unwanted software which it 'drops' and installs on the affected system. Commonly, the dropper installs a backdoor which allows remote, surreptitious access to infected systems. This backdoor may then be used by remote attackers to upload and install further malicious or potentially unwanted software on the system.

PWS:Win32/Zbot.gen!AP

This password-stealing trojan can record which keys you press and send this information to a malicious hacker.

This can include your online activity, like visits to banking websites.

Detected item	Alert level	Date
TrojanDropper:Win32/Bunitu	Severe	21/05/2014 1:49 PM
PWS:Win32/Zbot	Severe	21/05/2014 11:52 AM
Trojan:Win32/Alureon.GQ	Severe	21/05/2014 11:51 AM
Worm:Win32/Gamarue.I	Severe	21/05/2014 10:21 AM

TrojanDropper:Win32/Bunitu

This threat is classified as a trojan dropper. As its name suggests, a dropper trojan contains malicious or potentially unwanted software which it 'drops' and installs on the affected system. Commonly, the dropper installs a backdoor which allows remote, surreptitious access to infected systems. This backdoor may then be used by remote attackers to upload and install further malicious or potentially unwanted software on the system.

Worm:Win32/Gamarue.I

This worm can download files onto your PC.

It also copies itself to any USB flash drives connected to your PC.

MORE RECENT ATTEMPTS TO PLACE A VIRUS IN MY COMPUTER FOR MAKING A COMPLAINT??

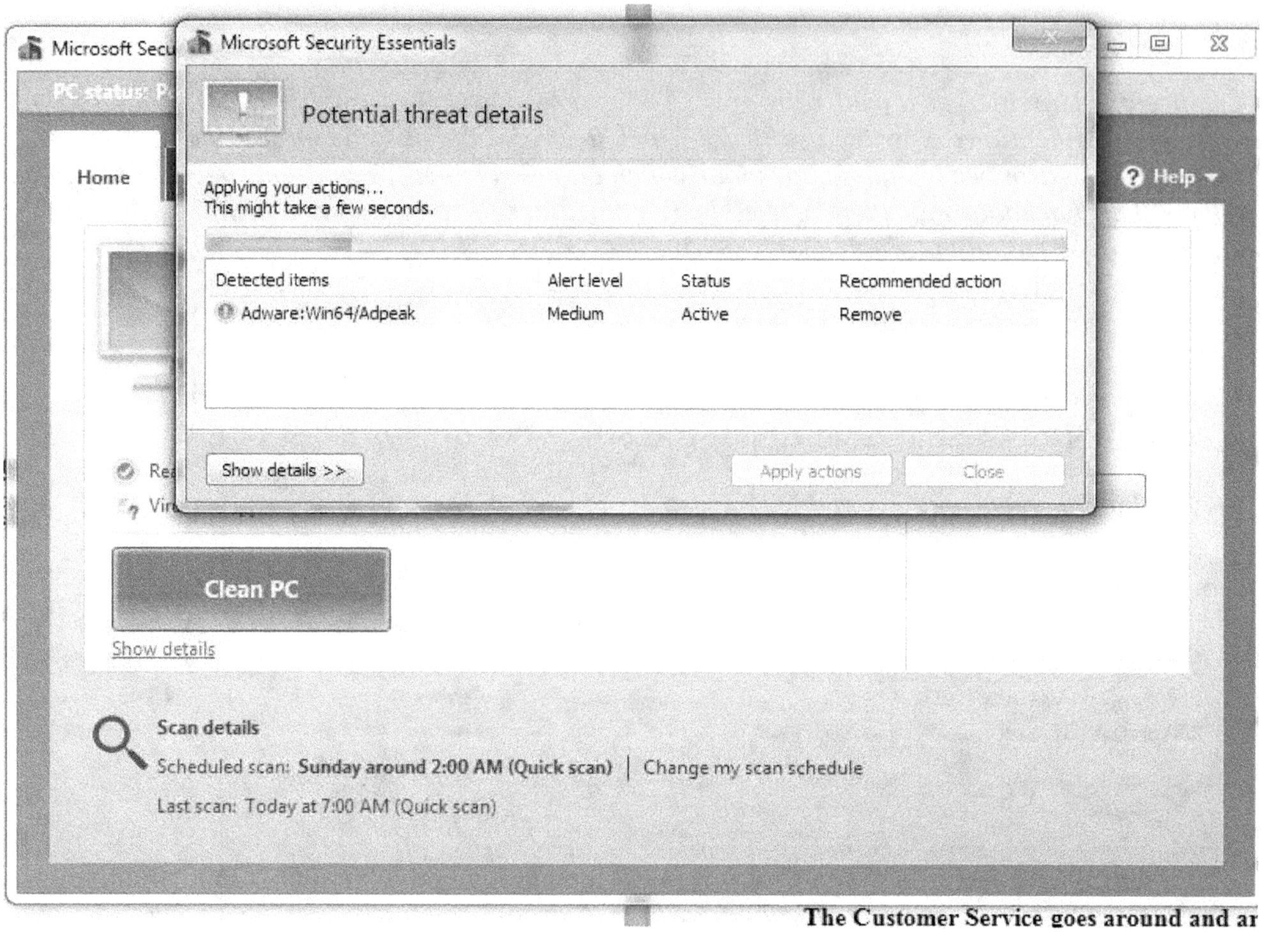

The Customer Service goes around and ar

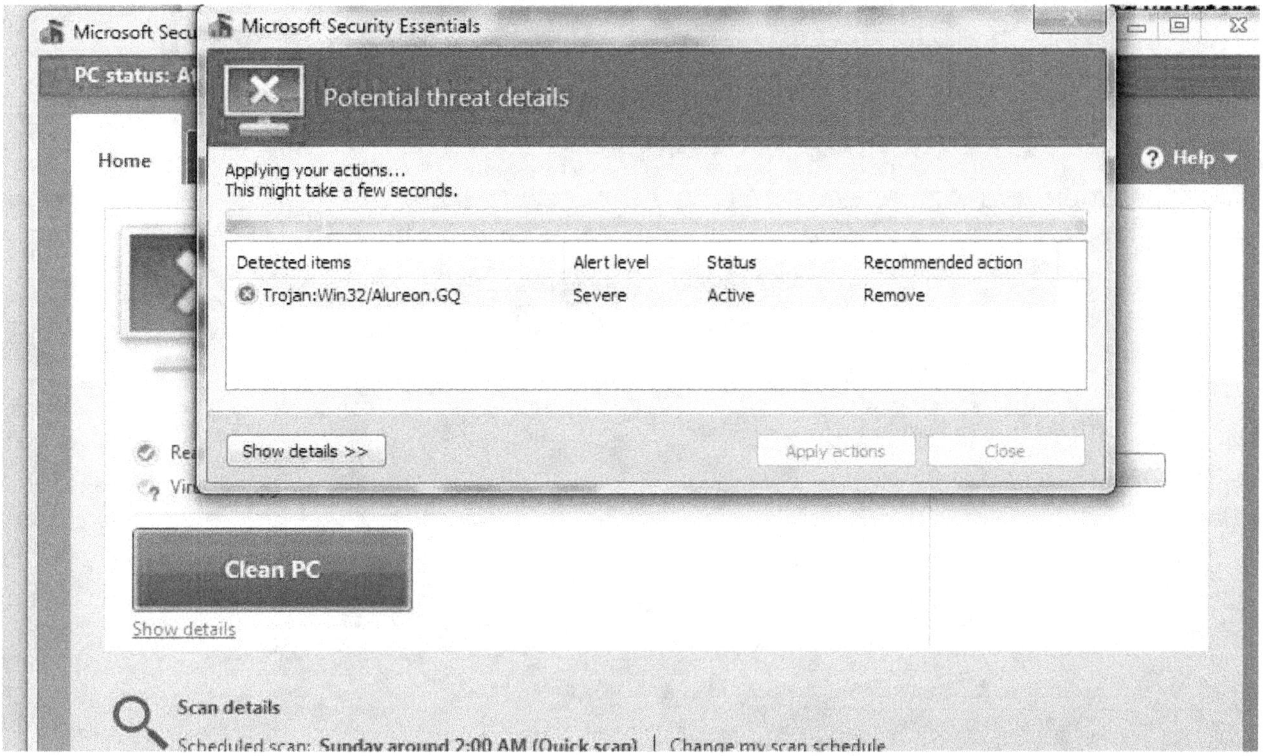

Is David Langtry, Canadian Human Rights Commissioner, more malicious than the LIARS he has working for him: Nicole Bomberg, Lorisa Stein and now Marie Josee Frenette_in retaliation for complaint about CHRC liars, in their attempts to stifle my complaint about Mental Disability [caused by RCMP illegal acts] Employment Discrimination???

CANADIAN HUMAN RIGHTS COMMISSION | COMMISSION CANADIENNE DES DROITS DE LA PERSONNE

CONTACT INFORMATION

YOUR CONTACT INFORMATION (YOU ARE THE COMPLAINANT)

Your first name	Your last name
Mailing ...	
Town or cit...	...de
Home phon... (include are...	...ber ...area code)
Your ...	
At which number ... Home ... Work ... Cell	
Please check here if your phone is a TTY (Text Telephone) ☐ Do you have any special needs related to ... disability that the Commission should know about, such as a specific format for communic... with you?	

I AM AGE 67, AND UNABLE TO WRITE THAT WELL, SO MY INFO IS PRIN...

, BA, BSW, MA
former federal peace officer
PTSD Disability Pensioner
Old Age Pensioner

YOUR ALTERNATE CONTACT'S INFORMATION

Please provide the contact information of the person that you would like contacted in the event that the Commission cannot reach you. Preferably, this should be a family member or friend who does not live with you.

Name of your alternate contact		Relation to you	
Mailing address			
Town or city		Province	Postal code
Home phone number (include area code)	Work phone number (include area code)	Cell phone number (include area code)	Fax number (include area code)

YOUR REPRESENTATIVE'S CONTACT INFORMATION

You do not need to hire a lawyer or other representative to file a complaint. If you do choose to hire a lawyer, please provide the following contact information.

If any of your personal contact information changes during the complaint process, it is your responsibility to inform the Canadian Human Rights Commission (the Commission).

If the Commission cannot reach you because you did not provide your current mailing address, your file may be closed

Name of your representative		Firm	
Mailing address			
Town or city		Province	Postal code
Work phone number *(include area code)*	Cell phone number *(include area code)*	Fax number *(include area code)*	Email address

ORGANIZATION YOUR COMPLAINT IS AGAINST

(THIS IS THE RESPONDENT)

If there is more than one respondent, you must file a separate complaint against each respondent.

I AM AGE 67, AND UNABLE TO WRITE THAT WELL, SO MY INFO IS PRINTED

RE: Retaliation for making an initial complaint to the CHRC, and this current Complaint against the Canadian Human Rights Commission for Retaliation for making the first complaint – A Discrimination Violation under your own Act:

☑ Retaliation for having filed a previous complaint under the Canadian Human Rights Act

RE: Marie Josee Frenette, CHRC Agent – You lied in your correspondence to me dated 12 May, 2014

You lied in your correspondence to me dated 12 May, 2014 when you said I had never made a Canadian Human Rights Commission complaint.

GRIEVANCE OR OTHER REDRESS PROCEDURES

According to the Canadian Human Rights Act, the Commission may decide not to deal with your complaint until you have exhausted all other redress procedures. These procedures may be available through a union or through other Acts of Parliament. Please provide the following information:

What actions have you taken so far to deal with this problem? *Select only those that apply.*

- ☐ Grievance
- ☐ Internal complaint
- ☐ Complaint under the *Canada Labour Code*
- ☐ Other ______

What is the status of these actions? *Select only those that apply.*

- ☐ Complaint or grievance filed
- ☐ Currently proceeding
- ☐ Waiting for arbitration
- ☐ Final decision rendered
- ☐ Other ______

None

Are you a member of a trade union or equivalent? ☐ Yes ☒ No

If **yes**, please provide the following information:

Name of your trade union or equivalent			
Mailing address			
Town or city		Province	Postal code
Name of your union representative			
Work phone number *(include area code)*	Cell phone number *(include area code)*	Fax number *(include area code)*	Email address

I hereby give permission to the Commission to contact my trade union or equivalent regarding my grievance.

Complainant's signature ______ **Date** 21 May 2014

COMPLAINT FORM

For Office Use Only: File Number

Your name *(You are the complainant)*

First : I AM AGE 67, AND UNABLE TO WRITE THAT WELL, SO MY INFO IS PRINTED , BA, BSW, MA *former federal peace officer, PTSD Disability Pensioner, Old Age Pensioner*

Who are you complaining against? *(This is the respondent)*
(If your complaint is accepted, the Commission will send a copy of this complaint to the respondent.)

I AM AGE 67, AND UNABLE TO WRITE THAT WELL, SO MY INFO IS PRINTED **RE: Retaliation for making an initial complaint to the CHRC, and this current Complaint against the Canadian Human Rights Commission for Retaliation**

Identify the area(s) in which you believe the discrimination took place:
Please select only those areas that apply to this complaint.

- ☐ Goods, services, facilities or accommodation
- ☐ Commercial premises or residential accommodation
- ☒ Employment
- ☐ Employment applications or advertisements
- ☐ Membership in a trade union or employee organization
- ☒ Discriminatory policy or practice
- ☐ Equal wages
- ☐ Publication of discriminatory notices, signs, symbols, emblems or other representations
- ☒ Hate messages
- ☒ Harassment
- ☒ Retaliation for having filed a previous complaint under the *Canadian Human Rights Act*

Identify the ground(s) of discrimination that you believe apply:
Please select only those grounds that apply to this complaint.

☐ Race	☐ Sex (includes pregnancy and childbirth)
☐ National or ethnic origin	☐ Sexual orientation
☐ Colour	☐ Marital status
☐ Religion	☐ Family status
☐ Age	☐ Conviction for which a pardon has been granted
☒ Disability	

Please select the box that applies to you

- [x] Canadian citizen
- [ ] Permanent resident
- [ ] In Canada on a Visa as a visitor, student or temporary foreign worker

(If none of these apply to you, you may not have status to file a complaint. In such a case, call the Commission to talk to an officer before submitting a complaint.)

In what city and province (or territory) did these events happen? (If the events took place ... Canada, ... officer before submitting a complaint.)

I AM AGE 67, AND UNABLE TO WRITE THAT WELL, SO MY INFO IS PRINTED
Canadian Penitentiary Employer, Mountain Prison, Canadian Human Rights Complaint – Nicole Bomberg, Lorisa Stein – British Columbia

When did the discrimination take place? Give the start date and the ... events. If the discrimination is still happening, select "ongoing".

The Commission can refuse to deal with a complaint that is filed <u>more than one year</u> after the alleged discrimination took place.

Start date (...)	
...	☒ Ongoing

I AM AGE 67, AND UNABLE TO WRITE THAT WELL, SO MY INFO IS PRINTED
Canadian Human Rights Complaint – lies by Nicole Bomberg, Lorisa Stein – British Columbia 1976, 1979,
Canadian Human Rights Complaint – lies by Marie Josee Frenette 12 May, 2014 - Ottawa

Write a statement to supp... ...llowing information:

- Who discriminated against ... Give the full names of the people involv... complaint.
- What happened? Were you treated differently from oth... ...dates of each event.
- Did this treatment have a negative effect on you? How were you affected?
- For each ground that you checked above, please give details. For example, if you checked race, please indicate your race. Explain how you were discriminated against based on each ground.

Instructions:
Write out your allegations in the box below. You cannot save this document electronically. If you exit the form, you will lose your data. You may wish to type out your allegations using a word processor, then copy and paste them into the box below. The text must not be more than 84 characters per line of text including blank spaces and a maximum of 114 lines of text including any returns (empty lines). Do not attach any other documents to the complaint. If your complaint is accepted, you may be asked for these documents at a later date. Complaints that are not in this format may be returned.

(See the last pages.)

I AM AGE 67, AND UNABLE TO WRITE THAT WELL, SO MY INFO IS PRINTED
SEE ATTACHED BOOKLET EXPLAINING COMPLAINT:

Canadian Human Rights Commission Liars, Nicole Bomber, Lorisa Stein and now Marie Josee Frenette!

Retaliation against Terry Mallenby by Canadian Human Rights Commission for making an initial complaint about Mental Disability Employment Discrimination!

Chapter 4

I did not know what it was called, but I was compelled to write!

My writing about personal matters occurred after 1976!

In those days, I didn't know what the medical diagnosis was?

I had been approved for a Canadian "(mental) disability pension" around 1979 for illegal acts and harassment by the Royal Canadian Mounted Police / RCMP Staff Sgt John Thomas Randle and other but I did not know the diagnosis [see Item #1 below]?

It was not until much later when I realized my compulsion to write was due to a need to reduce stress for PTSD – Chronic Type AND Social Phobia when my Canadian "(mental) disability pension" was renewed in 1998 [see Item #2 below].

And, as further found out in 2013, recent studies, including one by Gail Ironson, MD, PhD, from the University of Miami, suspected that writing about trauma could reduce PTSD symptoms and depression.

The name of this writing was Cognitive Processing Therapy:

Cognitive Processing Therapy, Matthew Tull, PhD
April 17, 2013:

Writing Proves to Be Therapeutic for Post-Traumatic Stress. Dutch researchers found that writing therapy "resulted in significant and substantial short-term reductions" of PTS and comorbid depression.

These conflicts are called "stuck points" and are addressed through, among other techniques, writing about the traumatic event.

> *Mr.X. : Has had Post Traumatic Stress Disorder for 40 years*
> [THIS BOOK WAS SUPPRESSED BY THE RCMP BECAUSE IT REFERRED TO THE ILLEGAL ACTS OF RCMP Staff Sgt John Thomas Randle]

Another event in 1975 that had a profound effect on Mr.X. was the death of fellow Classification Officer Mary Steinhauser and the apparent cover-up by the Canadian Government of her apparent purposeful murder.

> *Was Mary Steinhauser Murdered? Did the Canadian Government try to cover-up?*
> *http://www.amazon.com/Was-Mary-Steinhauser-Murdered-Government/dp/1475153791/ref=sr_1_1?s=books&ie=UTF8&qid=1393411341&sr=1-1&keywords=Mary+Steinhauser*
> [THIS BOOK WAS SUPPRESSED BY THE CANADIAN GOVRNMENT BECAUSE IT WAS EMBARRASING TO Canadian Prime Minister Stephen Harper]

A Preponderance of Evidence Identifies the RCMP [RCMP Commissioner Robert Paulson] and the Canadian Government [Prime Minister Stephen Harper] as suppressing the "therapeutic" writings of Mr.X. in his efforts to deal with his Post Traumatic Stress – Chronic Type duly identified and ratified by the Canada Pension Plan, resulting in Mr.X. receiving a [mental] disability pension for years.

This interference to Mr.X. 's "therapeutic writings" being suppressed by the RCMP [RCMP Commissioner Robert Paulson] and the Canadian Government [Prime Minister Stephen Harper] is a direct violation of the Canadian Human Rights Act, the Canadian Charter of Rights and Freedoms, including the Universal Declaration of Human Rights and forms part of the known facts in my complaint to the Canadian Human Rights Commission.

The facts of that Federal Court Action T-1131-83 include:

1976 Coroner's Inquest held in Squamish, British Columbia, Canada ruled the homicide was by Person or Persons Unknown [see below].

Mr.X. was age 28!

Forced Retirement at age 28: Because of Royal Canadian Mounted Police Lies
*http://www.amazon.com/Forced-Retirement-age-28-Canadian/dp/1481129082/ref=sr_1_1?s=books&ie=UTF8&qid=1393409553&sr=1-*1&keywords=forced+retirement+at+age+28

This book suppressed by RCMP Commissioner Robert Paulson and Canadian Prime Minister Stephen Harper – a preponderance of evidence points to these two as the culprits!

Who else would want to suppress it?

After all, they all had about the lies by RCMP Staff Sgt John Thomas Randle in them!

RCMP S/Sgt John Thomas Randle lies at the 1976 Coroner's

Inquest held in Squamish, British Columbia, Canada falsely stating the husband was an "unwilling witness" so the RCMP could arrest him?

The only problem is that because of RCMP S/Sgt John Thomas Randle lies, Mr.X. missed his wife's funeral!!

You can imagine the anguish this caused Mr.X. !!

Mr.X. will hate the RCMP until the day he dies!

And to prove that RCMP Staff Sgt John Thomas Randle is a big, fat liar and a "bloody arse hole" – Mr.X. used Randle's big fat lies to successfully sue the Queen of England, the Canada Government and the Royal Canadian Mounted Police including RCMP Staff Sgt John Thomas Randle!!

1976 Coroner's Inquest held in Squamish, British Columbia, Canada ruled the homicide was by Person or Persons Unknown

HOMICIDE: By Person or Persons Unknown: RCMP S/Sgt John Thomas Randle?
http://www.amazon.com/HOMICIDE-Person-Persons-Thomas-Randle/dp/1467919578/ref=sr_1_34?s=books&ie=UTF8&qid=1322848862&sr=1-34

This book suppressed by RCMP Commissioner Robert Paulson and Canadian Prime Minister Stephen Harper – a preponderance of evidence points to these two as the culprits!

Who else would want to suppress it?

After all, they all had about the lies by RCMP Staff Sgt John Thomas Randle in them!

The Coroner apologized to Mr.X. for listening to the RCMP / RCMP Staff Sgt John Thomas Randle that he was an "unwilling witness"!

In 2012, 2013 and currently in 2014 the RCMP, RCMP Commissioner Robert Paulson and the Canadian Government, Prime Minister Stephen Harper has had these same 1976 RCMP S/Sgt John Thomas Randle lies that Mr.X. was an "unwilling witness" uploaded to the Internet as payback for successfully suing the Royal Canadian Mounted Police over their lies and receiving a $275,000 out of court settlement!

In 2012, 2013 and currently in 2014 the RCMP, RCMP Commissioner Robert Paulson and the Canadian Government, Prime Minister Stephen Harper has had these same 1976 RCMP S/Sgt John Thomas Randle lies that Mr.X. was an "unwilling witness" uploaded to the as payback for writing about these illegal acts and lies by the Royal Canadian Mounted Police:

Mr.X. Successfully Sued the RCMP: Bob Paulson has 40 year old lies uploaded to the internet as RCMP payback

Stephen Harper, Another Big Sucky Baby: Uploads 40 year old RCMP lies, as payback

Mr.X. Successfully Sued the RCMP: Sanfu Chen uploads 40 year old RCMP lies as payback

Mr.X. Successfully Sued the RCMP: Does Rebecca Aldous or David Burke help upload 40 year old RCMP lies as payback

Forced Retirement at age 28: Because of Royal Canadian Mounted Police Lies

All these books have been suppressed by RCMP Commissioner Robert Paulson and Canadian Prime Minister Stephen Harper – a preponderance of evidence points to these two as the culprits!

Who else would want to suppress them?

After all, they all had about the lies by RCMP Staff Sgt John Thomas Randle in them!

1979 RCMP S/Sgt John Thomas Randle writes a letter saying that Mr.X. was a "murderer" and a copy is given to John Gomery to make sure Mr.X. remained unemployed

1979 M.J. Hauser of the Correctional Service of Canada in memo(s) also says that Mr.X. was a "murderer" to make sure he remained unemployed

1979 Nicole Bomberg of the Canadian Human Rights Commission in memo(s) also says that Mr.X. was a "murderer" to make sure he remained unemployed and this lie was used by Nicole Bomberg to not properly investigate the initial Human Rights Complaint based on lack of work with Canadian Penitentiary Services based on mental disability PTSD Chronic Type based on RCMP S/Sgt John Thomas Randle's lies – Nicole Bomberg lied so as to not embarrass the RCMP!

1979 Lorisa Stein of the Canadian Human Rights Commission in memo(s) also says that Mr.X. was a "murderer" to make sure he remained unemployed and this lie was used by Lorisa Stein to not properly investigate the initial Human Rights Complaint based on lack of work with Canadian Penitentiary Services based on mental disability PTSD Chronic Type based on RCMP S/Sgt John Thomas Randle's lies – Lorisa Stein lied so as to not embarrass the RCMP!

Mr.X. had heard through the "grape-vine" that Lorisa Stein had attended Queen's University and did find this about a Lisa Stein in Toronto, Ontario, Canada:

Lorisa Stein, Family Law Lawyer
150 York Street, Suite 800
Toronto,Ontario MSH 3S5
Fax: (416) 596-0599
Phone: 416 596- 8081

I attended Queen's University for my law degree, Carleton University and University of Toronto for my Master's degree in Political Sciences (Public Policy), and Western University and Universidad Iberoamericana for my Honours BA. Earning three degrees attending seven universities in five cities over 15 years shows my commitment, determination and dedication to following my dreams.

I am a member of the Law Society of Upper Canada, the Board of Directors of Collaborative Practice Toronto, the Association of Family and Conciliation Courts (AFCC), and the International Academy of Collaborative Practitioners (IACP).

Mr.X. wrote to this Lorisa Stein asking where she got the information from that Mr.X. was a "murderer" as cited in her Canadian Human Rights Commission in memo(s) – Mr. X received no reply from Lisa Stein!

2014 CHRC agent Marie Josee Frenette lied in her correspondence to me dated 12 May, 2014 when she said I had never made a Canadian Human Rights Commission complaint [against the RCMP].

As such, is she one of those psychopathic liars Oxford professor Kevin Dutton speaks about?

DAVID LANGTRY – YOU SEEM TO HAVE A LOT OF LIARS WORKING FOR YOU???

Mr.X. successfully sued RCMP!

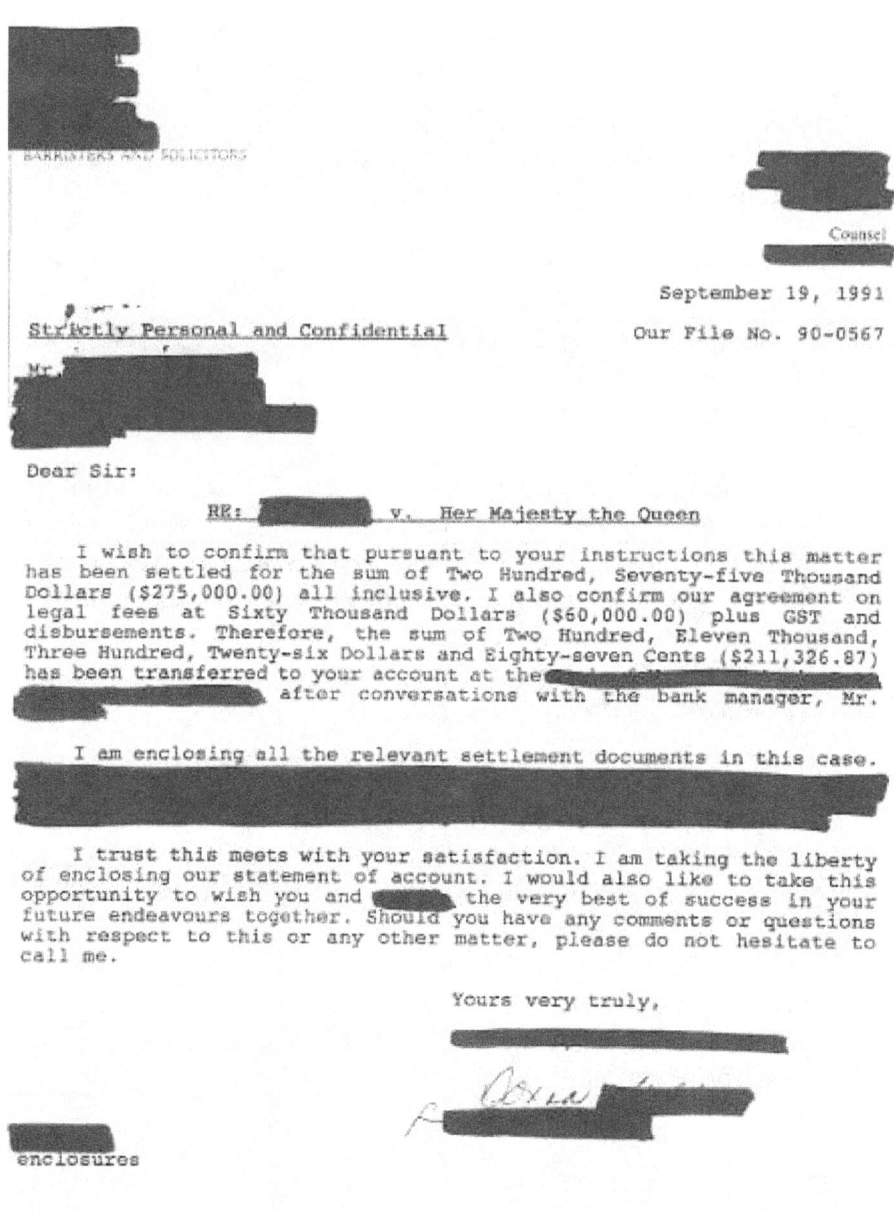

[redacted]
BARRISTERS AND SOLICITORS

[redacted]
Counsel
[redacted]

September 19, 1991

Strictly Personal and Confidential

Our File No. 90-0567

Mr. [redacted]

Dear Sir:

RE: [redacted] v. Her Majesty the Queen

I wish to confirm that pursuant to your instructions this matter has been settled for the sum of Two Hundred, Seventy-five Thousand Dollars ($275,000.00) all inclusive. I also confirm our agreement on legal fees at Sixty Thousand Dollars ($60,000.00) plus GST and disbursements. Therefore, the sum of Two Hundred, Eleven Thousand, Three Hundred, Twenty-six Dollars and Eighty-seven Cents ($211,326.87) has been transferred to your account at the [redacted] after conversations with the bank manager, Mr. [redacted]

I am enclosing all the relevant settlement documents in this case. [redacted]

I trust this meets with your satisfaction. I am taking the liberty of enclosing our statement of account. I would also like to take this opportunity to wish you and [redacted] the very best of success in your future endeavours together. Should you have any comments or questions with respect to this or any other matter, please do not hesitate to call me.

Yours very truly,

[redacted]

[redacted]

[redacted]
enclosures

[redacted] Ottawa, Ontario [redacted] Fax: (613) [redacted] Telephone: (613) [redacted]

Mr.X. successfully sued RCMP!

18 '91 12:38 JUSTICE CANADA MONTREAL P.3/8

No: T-1131-83

IN THE FEDERAL COURT OF CANADA
TRIAL DIVISION

BETWEEN:

[redacted],

and

Plaintiffs

AND:

HER MAJESTY THE QUEEN, ROYAL CANADIAN
MOUNTED POLICE and J.I. RANDLE,

Defendants

DECLARATION OF SETTLEMENT

The parties, by their counsel, hereby declare that the present case has now been settled, each party paying its own costs.

SIGNED in Montreal, this ____
day of September 1991

Mr.X. successfully sued RCMP!

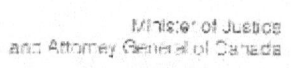

Minister of Justice
and Attorney General of Canada

CANADA

Ministre de la Justice
et Procureure générale du Canada

A. Kim Campbell, P.C., Q.C., M.P./c.p., c.r., députée

OCT 15 1991

Mr. David Kilgour, M.P.
House of Commons
Ottawa, K1A 0A6

Dear Mr. Kilgour:

Thank you for your letter of August 21, 1991, concerning Mr. [redacted].

I have been informed that Treasury Board has now approved the proposed settlement and that the cheque is being prepared. The cheque as well as release documents will be forwarded to Mr. [redacted] counsel in the very near future, if this has not already been done.

Yours sincerely,

A. Kim Campbell

RECEIVED - REÇU
OCT 18 1991
HOUSE OF COMMONS
Chambre des Communes

Ottawa, Canada K1A 0H8

Here in black and white is an up-to-date diagnoses for Mr. X with a multitude of disorders as a consequence of RCMP and Federal Government illegal acts, harassment and other abuse – which Nicole Bomberg and Lorisa Stein of the Canadian Human Rights Commission purposefully ignored with their lies as the reason Mr.X. was not be employed by the Canadian Penitentiary Service as per the initial Canadian Human Rights Commission complaint!

Author's note: Anyone who has to identify a loved-one in the morgue can appreciate the horror, grief, anger one experiences?

September 24th, 1996

The Medical Advisor
Income Security Programs
333 River Rd
Ottawa, Ontario
K1A 9Z9

OCT 7 1996

Dear Sir or Madame:

Re:

I am writing a letter on behalf of one of my patients who suffers from a grievous mental malady. He has been previously accepted for CPP disability.

His case is complicated. He is a very accomplished gentleman who has two advanced degrees including a Ph.D. and yet cannot work. He spends his time largely sequestered at home writing notes and letters and suffers extreme anxiety if he attempts to go outside.

He is very secretive about events that happened in the past but evidently he sustained a major personal loss in 1976 and ever since then has never recovered. He has paranoid ideas and symptoms of marked anxiety. I have been treating him as best I could as a family physician but felt his symptoms were aggravated and complicated enough that I referred him to a psychiatrist.

suffers from many symptoms of post-traumatic stress disorder and unresolved grief.....fear, guilt, horror, dreams of traumatic content, social avoidancy, decreased interest, impaired memory, irritability, anger, increased vigilance, sense of futility regarding the future, some paranoid ideations.

Here in black and white is an up-to-date diagnoses for Mr. X with a multitude of disorders as a consequence of RCMP and Federal Government illegal acts, harassment and other abuse – which Nicole Bomberg and Lorisa Stein of the Canadian Human Rights Commission purposefully ignored with their lies as the reason Mr.X. was not be employed by the Canadian Penitentiary Service as per the initial Canadian Human Rights Commission complaint!

Anyone who has to identify a loved-one in the morgue can appreciate the horror, grief, anger one experiences?

October 17, 1996

FRANCOISE LeBLANC, R.N., B.A.,
DISABILITY OPERATIONS DIVISION
333 RIVER ROAD
OTTAWA, CANADA K1A 0L1

RE:

Dear Francoise,

Thank you for your letter of October 1, 1996

gives a 20 year history of Post-Traumatic Stress Disorder following the homicide of a colleague in a prison uprising and also the murder in 1976. I believe you are well aware of these events and that was falsely accused of the latter crime. The effect on his family relationships and on him are also well documented. has become very suspicious of others especially Government agencies and is somewhat paranoid. This paranoia has made it difficult for him to accept psychological help as a degree of trust is almost essential. He seems to have made numerous attempts to improve his occupational situation, but his difficulties dealing with others always overwhelm him.

When seen, exhibited and described numerous signs and symptoms of Post-Traumatic Stress Disorder including marked agitation whenever the subject of the murder loomed. He described fear, guilt and horror, traumatic dreams, social avoidance, loss of interest, poor memory for details of the murder, irritability, anger, increased vigilance, a sense of futility re. the future, difficulties with emotional involvement, and arousal by recollections of the trauma including those precipitated by news stories of similar events. In interviews, he is often tearful ,distraught and agitated.

Diagnostically, he has 1) Post-Traumatic Stress Disorder -Chronic Type
2) Social Phobia -secondary to 1)

Here in black and white is an up-to-date diagnoses for Mr. X with a multitude of disorders as a consequence of RCMP and Federal Government illegal acts, harassment and other abuse – which Nicole Bomberg and Lorisa Stein of the Canadian Human Rights Commission purposefully ignored with their lies as the reason Mr.X. was not be employed by the Canadian Penitentiary Service as per the initial Canadian Human Rights Commission complaint!

April 1, 1998

To: Mr. Denis Duhamel
Tower A, 11th floor
Place Vanier

From: Dr. N. Kanjilal
Medical Advisor

Subject:

As per your request, I reviewed the file of to determine the basis for granting him the disability benefits.

You are well aware that we are guided by the CPP Legislation which states that a person must be suffering from a physical and/or mental disability which is both severe and prolonged to be eligible to receive disability benefits. Severe means that the person must be incapable of pursuing any substantially gainful occupation regularly. Prolonged means that the incapacity to work at any substantially gainful occupation will likely be long continued and of indefinite duration. To assess such disability we have to ascertain the limiting loss or absence of the capacity to meet the occupational demands according to the regulatory requirements described above.

seems to have satisfied the legislation and in our judgement he is incapable to carry out any occupational demands.

will be well advised to consult his treating physicians if he wishes to find out about any particular medical condition, who will be in a better position to explain his specific question.

Hope this answers some of your problems. Please do not hesitate to contact me should you need any other information.

Dr. N. Kanjilal
Tel: 952-3620

Chapter 5

An outright lie by Canadian Human Rights Commission agent Marie Josee Frenette in 2014 saying I had never made a CHRC complaint against the RCMP!

Canadian human rights commission | Commission canadienne des droits de la personne

Resolution Services Division | Division des services de règlement

MAY 12 2014

PROTECTED

File number: 11400726

Mr. .

Dear Mr.

This letter is further to your correspondence of March 20, April 17 and April 20, 2014, addressed to Acting Chief Commissioner David Langtry, and your telephone conversation on April 22, 2014, with Mr. Jamie Masters, Early Resolution Advisor regarding your concerns with a number of federal government departments.

Please note that given his position as Acting Chief Commissioner, it is not appropriate for Acting Chief Commissioner Langtry to respond to correspondence dealing with complaints as he may be called upon to render a decision on a specific file. For this reason, I am responding on his behalf.

Both Mr. Masters and I have reviewed your complaints and related documentation carefully. Unfortunately, they cannot be accepted because they do not meet the requirements of a complaint under the *Canadian Human Rights Act* (CHRA). As such, we have closed your file.

What should I do now?

You can submit new complaint forms if you can fix whatever was missing or unclear in your first complaint form.

What do I need to fix?

1. **You have not identified a discriminatory practice outlined in sections 5-14.1 of the Act**

As Mr. Masters informed you in your conversation, on April 22, 2014:

- The Squamish Public Library publishing archived copies of the now-defunct *Squamish Times* newspaper online does not constitute a discriminatory practice under the CHRA.
- There are not reasonable grounds to believe that the online publication of the now-defunct *Squamish Times* newspaper is a move by the RCMP and other government agencies to retaliate against you for an out-of-court settlement you reached with the

.../2

344 Slater Street, Ottawa, Ontario K1A 1E1
344, rue Slater, Ottawa (Ontario) K1A 1E1
Toll-free/Sans frais 1-888-214-1090, TTY/ATS 1-888-643-3304, Fax/Téléc. (613) 996-9661
www.chrc-ccdp.gc.ca

RCMP in the 1990s. In fact, the article from *Pique News Magazine* that you provided in your documentation clearly indicates this was a project undertaken by the Squamish Public Library to continue building its digital archives collection. While you have developed a theory as to how all of the named departments are working in concert against you, on their face these allegations amount to speculation and bald assertions.

- More than speculation is needed to file a complaint. The courts have been clear that "reasonable grounds" require more than just a statement or bald assertion that the conduct is discriminatory. There is an obligation on the part of the complainant to demonstrate that a "reasonable person" in the same circumstances would believe that the policies or practices complained of are discriminatory.

2. You have not shown a link between the alleged discriminatory act(s) and the ground(s) of discrimination.

While you have identified as a person with a disability, you have not made a link between your disability and any of the alleged actions by the PMO, the RCMP, the Copyright Board of Canada, the Privacy Commission of Canada or the Canadian Human Rights Commission. Similarly, you have not made a link to the ground of family status for the complaints you have made on behalf of your family members.

3. A complaint can be no more than three (3) letter-sized pages.

The material you have sent us clearly exceeds the three (3) page limit for a complaint to the Commission. Furthermore, each 3 page complaint must stand on its own. You cannot make reference to attachments and/or previous letters you have sent to the Commission as none of these documents will be sent to the respondents when / if the Commission notifies them of your complaints.

As an aside, it is important that you avoid altering the Commission's complaint kit. Your three (3) page narrative of the complaint must be attached to the complaint kit, not pasted over it.

4. No retaliation as defined in the CHRA

CHRC FALSE STATEMENT

You also allege that the PMO, the RCMP, the Copyright Board of Canada, the Privacy Commission of Canada and the Canadian Human Rights Commission have retaliated against you for the out-of-court settlement you reached with the RCMP in the 1990s. Please note that retaliation in the context of the CHRA refers to situations where a respondent engages in some sort of adverse treatment or threats against a complainant for making a previous CHRC complaint against the same respondent. As you have never filed a formal CHRC complaint against the PMO, the RCMP, the Copyright Board of Canada, the Privacy Commission of Canada or the Canadian Human Rights Commission, by definition none of them could have committed retaliation as outlined in the CHRA.

.../3

344 Slater Street, Ottawa, Ontario K1A 1E1
344, rue Slater, Ottawa (Ontario) K1A 1E1
Toll-free/Sans frais 1-888-214-1090, TTY/ATS 1-888-643-3304, Fax/Téléc. (613) 996-9661
www.chrc-ccdp.gc.ca

Finally, your allegations refer to violations of the *Charter of Rights and Freedoms* and the *Universal Declaration of Human Rights* as well as the CHRA. Please note that the Commission only has the legal authority to deal with complaints under the CHRA. The Commission cannot address alleged violations of the *Charter of Rights and Freedoms* or non-compliance with the *Universal Declaration of Human Rights*.

Given that your complaints are unacceptable in their current form, I am returning the originals and all supporting documents to you and have not kept copies. In addition, I have enclosed some information to assist you should you wish to continue with your complaints. If you have any questions or need more information, please call Mr. Jamie Masters, Early Resolution Advisor at 613-943-9040 or call toll-free at 1-888-214-1090.

Yours sincerely,

Marie Josée Frenette
Early Resolution Team Leader

Encl. Original complaint forms and documentation
Instructions for Filing a Complaint

344 Slater Street, Ottawa, Ontario K1A 1E1
344, rue Slater, Ottawa (Ontario) K1A 1E1
Toll-free/Sans frais 1-888-214-1090, TTY/ATS 1-888-643-3304, Fax/Téléc. (613) 996-9661
www.chrc-ccdp.gc.ca

Recorded entries for T-1131-83

Court number information			
Court Number :	T-1131-83		
Style of Cause :	MR.X. ET AL v. THE QUEEN ET AL		
Proceeding Category :	Actions	Nature :	Others - Crown (v. Queen) [Actions]
Type of Action :	Undetermined		

2 records found for T-1131-83			
Doc	Date Filed	Office	Recorded Entry Summary
502	1992-01-27	Montréal	Settlement reached by all parties with regard to the present case received from Defendant filed on 27-JAN-1992
501	1992-01-27	Montréal	Minutes of Settlement filed on 27-JAN-1992

The last database update occurred on 2014-04-06 15:32

Chapter 6

Is RCMP S/Sgt John Thomas Randle one of the Psychopaths that Dr. Dutton from Oxford's Magdalen College speaks about?

David Langtry
Chief Commissioner
Canadian Human Rights Commission
344 Slater Street, 8th Floor
Ottawa, Ontario K1A 1E1
Toll Free: 1-888-214-1090
Fax: 613-996-9661
registrar@chrt-tcdp.gc.ca
communications@chrc-ccdp.gc.ca
library@chrc-ccdp.ca

I suggest you speak to that apparent PSYCHOPATH John Thomas Randle as to why Nicole Bomberg, Lorisa Stein and now Marie Josee Frenette feel they can lie with impunity???

Maybe you can get some help from that other apparent PSYCHOPATH Senator Larry Campbell, former RCMP officer and former Chief Coroner who says he doesn't give a shite about the Squamish murders:

Who to hell is Senator Larry W. Campbell that he doesn't care about the missing and murdered in Squamish, British Columbia?

This Larry Campbell has a long career of law enforcement and death investigation, yet with respect to the missing and murdered in Squamish, British Columbia he says -

> *On 2013-07-02, Larry Campbell sent an email to Mr. X*
>
> *The email was from Senator Larry Campbell - <Larry.Campbell@sen.parl.gc.ca>*
>
> *Senator Larry Campbell, who is a former RCMP officer, wrote –*
>
> *Yawn*
>
> *Squamish again*
>
> *Larry Campbell*

Here's the missing and murdered in Squamish, British Columbia, Canada that Senator Larry Campbell, former RCMP officer, doesn't give "two hoots" about:

SQUAMISH # 1

Oct. 29, '85: Rachel Turley, 20
Turley's body was found in a wooded area near Squamish. She had been sexually assaulted, beaten and strangled. Police say she was known to them as a Granville Mall "street person" who once worked as a prostitute.

A 2001 Vancouver Sun article listing the missing
http://www.highwayoftears.ca/missingbclist.htm

SQUAMISH # 2

Topic: 1970's Squamish, BC - possible connection between 3 murders?
Re: 1970's Squamish, BC - possible connection between 3 murders?
« Reply #20 on: August 02, 2011, 04:19:55 PM »

I'm sorry about your friend. Sadly there were so many serial killers in this area during that era, it hard to know for sure.

Unsolved Murders | Missing People Canada
http://www.unsolvedcanada.ca/index.php?topic=3091.15

SQUAMISH # 3

Re: Jodi Henrickson~17~missing~Bowen Island/Squamish~June 20,2009
« Reply #61 on: May 23, 2012, 11:55:54 AM »
Body found on Bowen Island
By Jane Seyd, North Shore News May 23, 2012 6:34 AM

POLICE investigating the discovery of a body in a bushy area of Bowen Island say the remains are likely not those of missing Squamish teen Jodi Henrickson.

"We don't feel it's connected to that case," said Sgt. Jennifer Pound, spokeswoman for the RCMP's Integrated Homicide Investigation Team. Pound said investigators ruled out that the body was Henrickson early on, although she declined to say how police did that.

Bowen Island RCMP were called out Friday at around 2 p.m. by a local resident who had discovered the body on his land, a wooded property in the 1,000 block of Harding Road.

An autopsy is to be performed Tuesday to try to identify the victim and the likely cause of death. Suicide remains a possibility, as does the chance that the body was dumped there.

"There are no obvious signs of injury," said Pound.

So far investigators have not confirmed whether the body - which was badly decomposed - is male or female. "We believe the body was there for quite some time," said Pound.

Lloyd Harding, who lives on Harding Road, said he was walking down to his mailbox with his son's dog at the end of last week when the Jack Russell terrier tried to drag him into the bush.

Harding said he noticed a bad smell in the area. "I thought someone had hit a deer he said."

Harding said he's walked right by the area where the body was found before but didn't see anything or notice any smell in the area before last week's spell of hot weather.

Police are currently checking missing persons reports to see if they can help identify the remains.

Henrickson, then 17, disappeared three years ago on June 20, 2009 after leaving a house party on Bowen Island with her ex-boyfriend Gavin Arnott. Neither Henrickson nor any signs of her have shown up since then, despite several searches by both police and volunteers.

Police have repeatedly said they think Henrickson met with foul play and never left the island.

Harding said the quiet community is "shocked and very concerned" by Friday's discovery.

jseyd@nsnews.com

http://www.nsnews.com/news/Body+found+Bowen+Island/6663655/story.html

Unsolved Murders | Missing People Canada
http://www.unsolvedcanada.ca/index.php?topic=2890.60

SQUAMISH # 4

Christopher Leo Turgeon | 3 | Missing Squamish BC | December 18, 1999
« on: July 17, 2011, 10:39:27 PM »
Case Number: 0000110

Missing Since: 18 December 1999
Missing From: Squamish, British Columbia, CANADA
Details: Christopher was abducted by his non-custodial mother, Lilia VAZQUEZ.
Missing Child:

Christopher Leo TURGEON
Date of Birth: 14 March 1996
Sex: Male
Hair: Brown
Eye: Brown
Height: 91 cm (36 feet, inches)
Weight: 19 kg (42 lb)
Additional Information: He has a mole on his lower lip on the right side. He speaks English and Spanish.
Christopher's photo is age-progressed to 7 years old.

May be in the company of:

Lilia Martinez VAZQUEZ
Date of Birth: 23 March 1974
Sex: Female
Hair: Brown
Eye: Brown
Height: 173 cm (68 feet, inches)
Weight: 50 kg (110 lb)
Additional Information: The abductor was born in Mexico. She speaks Spanish and English.
Alias(es): Lilia MARTINEZ, Lilia MARTINEZ VAZQUEZ, Lilia VASQUEZ

Relationship: Mother
http://www.ourmissingchildren.gc.ca/cgi-bin/case.pl?id=181&lang=eng

Unsolved Murders | Missing People Canada
http://www.unsolvedcanada.ca/index.php?topic=5195.0

SQUAMISH # 5

Re: 1950 - 1969 Unsolved Murders and Missing - Canada

« Reply #45 on: April 11, 2010, 06:18:24 PM »

Furry Creek, BC Okay, I am going to post some more of my findings, unfortunately, not much to find. I will post the info over a few posts. This first lot is not in the date sequence as originally listed. I may have found a common thread in these ones. Although they are listed as Squamish/Vancouver cases, when I looked at the death registration information on Ancestry.ca I found all of their locations of death were within 18km of a place called Furry Creek, BC. I have included one that was listed as Squamish as it seems to be in the same area. I am not sure if these young ladies actually died/were found near Furry Creek or if they were perhaps, from there, and therefore, their deaths were listed for that location. I have to break this one into two posts as the computer is fussing

1. 12 April 73 Helen Hopcroft, age 17, Vancouver
Her death was registered as 13 May 73, Furry Creek, BC
There was an obituary for her in the Winnipeg Free Press 7 June 73

2. 17 Feb 75 Gayle Rogers, Vancouver, BC
If it is the same young lady, found "Gail Sandra Rogers" Date of registered death, 7 Mar 75, she was born in 1949 so she was 26,
her death is registered as "Squamish, BC"

Unsolved Murders | Missing People Canada
http://www.unsolvedcanada.ca/index.php?topic=416.45

SQUAMISH # 6

Fraser Member
Posts: 120
« Reply #46 on: April 11, 2010, 06:27:30 PM »
Furry Creek cont'd

3. 25 Jan 75 Margie Melinda Blackwell, 21
Death registration: 25 Jan 75, place of death, Furry Creek, BC

4. 26 Feb 76 Ruth Gwendolyn Mallenby, 26, Squamish
Death Registration: "Ruth Gwendelyne Mallenby", 7 Mar 76 Lion's Bay, (18 km from Furry Creek, BC)

For everyone's consideration. If I find anymore with this link I will add them to this post.

Unsolved Murders | Missing People Canada
http://www.unsolvedcanada.ca/index.php?topic=416.45

SQUAMISH # 7

Sunday afternoon a group of hikers found a dead body near a hiking trail on the side of Mamquam Road in Squamish. "It appears the man was met with foul play," said spokeswoman Sgt. Jennifer Pound. "It does appear to be a homicide." Pound also refused to comment on media reports that the man's body was found beaten and duct-taped.

Kim Bolan has reported the identity of the body is that of William Woo from Surrey who was an associate of the East Vancouver hells angels but more recently went over to the other side. Now he's in a body bag. I wonder who the prime suspects are? If the East Vancouver chapter of the Hells angels contract a murder, that makes them a criminal organization guilty of murder. I don't know about the Duhre Daiquiris but Lotus, now there is some old school credibility right there. They are more than capable of professional payback.

Beaten and duck taped. Yeah that would imply foul play. It reminds me of two other cases in Squamish. One was a guy named Alex Larsen who was run over by a truck because he was lying in the middle of the road. It's so strange and tragic. Yes it's possible he got drunk or high and passed out. Yet we've never heard a word either way. We don't know if he was beaten and dumped there or if he was walking on the side of the road and a car hit him which was why he was lying in the middle of the road before the bus ran him over. The case comes to mind and I wish there was more pieces to that puzzle. They say he had made a decision to turn his life around. Just like Britney Irving. Tragic indeed.

Of course there's that other bizarre case in Squamish, the murder of Javan Luke Dowling. Three drug dealers were driving in a car in Vancouver. One of the drug dealers, shot one of the other drug dealers in the head and the third drug dealer watched the shooter cut off Dowling's head and dismembered his body. The two surviving drug dealers buried the body in two separate locations in Squamish. Mihaly Illes was alleged to be the shooter while Derrick Madinski helped him bury the body. Derrick Madinski went with Joe Brallic to LA where Joe was ripped off and murdered.

Meanwhile in that same original article about a new dead body being found in Squamish it later stated there was another shooting in Surrey near the corner of 111A Avenue and 146th Street at about 2: 40 a.m. on Sunday. It didn't even make it's own head line. Kinda sad. The point is violent crime is continuing and as the papers also report the court system is currently in crisis. That was before Harper's disproportionate crime bill sent the fragile system into chaos.

Gangsters Out Blog
http://gangstersout.blogspot.ca/2011/10/body-dumped-in-squamish.html

Chapter 7

These Are The Facts, 1976 to the Present!

THESE ARE THE FACTS COMMENCING IN 1976 BECAUSE OF RCMP PSYCHOPATH S/SGT JOHN THOMAS RANDLE'S LIES AND THOSE BY CHRC LIARS NICOLE BOMBERG & LORISA STEIN, TOGETHER WITH THE LIE BY CHRC MARIE JOSEE FRENETTE THAT I NEVER BEFORE MADE A CANADIAN HUMAN RIGHTS COMPLAINT:

Item #1

In recent studies, including one by Gail Ironson, MD, PhD, from the University of Miami, suspected that writing about trauma could reduce PTSD symptoms and depression.

Cognitive Processing Therapy, Matthew Tull, PhD
April 17, 2013:

Writing Proves to Be Therapeutic for Post-Traumatic Stress. Dutch researchers found that writing therapy "resulted in significant and substantial short-term reductions" of PTS and comorbid depression.

These conflicts are called "stuck points" and are addressed through, among other techniques, writing about the traumatic event.

> *Mr.X. : Has had Post Traumatic Stress Disorder for 40 years*
> [THIS SUPPRESSED BOOK IS AVAILABLE TO THE CHRC AS A PDF]

Another event in 1975 that had a profound effect on Mr.X. was the death of fellow Classification Officer Mary Steinhauser and the apparent cover-up by the Canadian Government of her apparent purposeful murder.

> *Was Mary Steinhauser Murdered? Did the Canadian Government try to cover-up? http://www.amazon.com/Was-Mary-Steinhauser-Murdered-Government/dp/1475153791/ref=sr_1_1?s=books&ie=UTF8&qid=1393411341&sr=1-1&keywords=Mary+Steinhauser*
> [THIS SUPPRESSED BOOK IS AVAILABLE TO THE CHRC AS A PDF]

There is no question in my mind that: Mary Steinhauser was purposefully shot
http://www.amazon.com/There-question-mind-that-purposefully/dp/1481978020/ref=sr_1_9?s=books&ie=UTF8&qid=1393411341&sr=1-9&keywords=Mary+Steinhauser
[THIS SUPPRESSED BOOK IS AVAILABLE TO THE CHRC AS A PDF]

As a "layman", part of dealing with his Post Traumatic Stress – Chronic Type Mr. X ironically took to writing about the RCMP false statements, harassment, illegal, acts:

Post-Traumatic Stress Disorder: Writing about it helps
http://www.amazon.com/Post-Traumatic-Stress-Disorder-Writing-about/dp/148114748X/ref=sr_1_3?s=books&ie=UTF8&qid=1393405643&sr=1-3&keywords=wallice+bellair+%22ptsd%22
[THIS SUPPRESSED BOOK IS AVAILABLE TO THE CHRC AS A PDF]

A Preponderance of Evidence Identifies the RCMP [RCMP Commissioner Robert Paulson] and the Canadian Government [Prime Minister Stephen Harper] as suppressing the "therapeutic" writings of Mr.X. in his efforts to deal with his Post Traumatic Stress – Chronic Type duly identified and ratified by the Canada Pension Plan, resulting in Mr.X. receiving a [mental] disability pension for years [see Appendices below].

This interference to Mr.X. 's "therapeutic writings" being suppressed by the RCMP [RCMP Commissioner Robert Paulson] and the Canadian Government [Prime Minister Stephen Harper] is a direct violation of the Canadian Human Rights Act, the Canadian Charter of Rights and Freedoms, including the Universal Declaration of Human Rights and forms part of the known facts in our joint complaint to the Canadian Human Rights Commission.

<u>Item # 2</u>

1976 Coroner's Inquest held in Squamish, British Columbia, Canada ruled the homicide was by Person or Persons Unknown [see Appendices below].

Mr.X. was age 28!

Forced Retirement at age 28: Because of Royal Canadian Mounted Police Lies
http://www.amazon.com/Forced-Retirement-age-28-Canadian/dp/1481129082/ref=sr_1_1?s=books&ie=UTF8&qid=1393409553&sr=1-1&keywords=forced+retirement+at+age+28
[THIS SUPPRESSED BOOK IS AVAILABLE TO THE CHRC AS A PDF]

The RCMP, the RCMP S/Sgt John Thomas Randle lies at the 1976 Coroner's Inquest held in Squamish, British Columbia, Canada falsely stating the husband was an "unwilling witness" so the RCMP could arrest him?

RCMP lie at 1976 Coroner Inquest: Ruth Mallenby homicide by Person or Persons Unknown
http://www.amazon.com/RCMP-lie-1976-Coroner-Inquest/dp/1480256234/ref=sr_1_1?s=books&ie=UTF8&qid=1362728904&sr=1-1&keywords=RCMP+LIES
[THIS SUPPRESSED BOOK IS AVAILABLE TO THE CHRC AS A PDF]

The only problem is that because of the RCMP, RCMP S/Sgt John Thomas Randle lies, Mr.X. missed his wife's funeral!!

You can imagine the anguish this caused Mr.X. !!

And to prove that RCMP Staff Sgt John Thomas Randle is a liar – Mr.X. used Randle's lies contained in a letter in 1979 by RCMP S/Sgt John Thomas Randle to successfully sue the Queen of England, the Canada Government and the Royal Canadian Mounted Police including RCMP Staff Sgt John Thomas Randle [see Appendices below].

1976 Coroner's Inquest held in Squamish, British Columbia, Canada ruled the homicide was by Person or Persons Unknown

HOMICIDE: By Person or Persons Unknown: RCMP S/Sgt John Thomas Randle?
http://www.amazon.com/HOMICIDE-Person-Persons-Thomas-Randle/dp/1467919578/ref=sr_1_34?s=books&ie=UTF8&qid=1322848862&sr=1-34
[THIS SUPPRESSED BOOK IS AVAILABLE TO THE CHRC AS A PDF]

The Coroner apologized to Mr.X. for listening to the RCMP / RCMP Staff Sgt John Thomas Randle that he was an "unwilling witness"!

Currently in 2014 a Preponderance of Evidence Identifies the RCMP [RCMP Commissioner Robert Paulson] and the Canadian Government [Prime Minister Stephen Harper] has had these same 1976 RCMP / RCMP S/Sgt John Thomas Randle lies that Mr.X. was an "unwilling witness" uploaded to the Internet as very apparent payback for Mr.X. successfully suing the Royal Canadian Mounted Police over RCMP S/Sgt John Thomas Randle 1979 letter where Mr.X. received a $275,000 out of court settlement to put a stop to all actions by the RCMP and the Canadian Government in their Canadian Human Rights Act violations, the Canadian Charter of Rights and Freedoms violations, their Universal Declaration of Human Rights and any other violations under any other legislation that may be applicable!

Mr.X. Successfully Sued the RCMP: Bob Paulson has 40 year old lies uploaded to internet as RCMP payback
[THIS SUPPRESSED BOOK IS AVAILABLE TO THE CHRC AS A PDF]

1979 Not satisfied with their lies in 1976, RCMP S/Sgt John Thomas Randle writes a letter saying that the husband was a "murderer" and a copy is given to John Gomery to make sure Mr.X. remained unemployed

RCMP S/Sgt John Thomas Randle "DEAD-BEAT DAD"?

In 2013, Mr.X. receives a phone call from Marshal S. purporting to be RCMP S/Sgt John Thomas Randle's son who Randle apparently abandoned at birth?

Although the young man only wanted to know Randle's medical history [typical of adopted children], apparently this RCMP S/Sgt John Thomas Randle told the young fellow to "piddle-off"?

Credence is given to Marshal S. because he mentioned that his friend from his boyhood days in Fort McMurray, Alberta - Brian Jean had apparently put him onto Mr.X. , because Mr.X. had written about RCMP Randle!

In fact an email from Brian Jean, Member of Parliament, confirmed this boyhood friendship:

+ Marshall S

Frances Jean sent it to me on **Jan 28, 2014, 6:10 PM**

From: Frances Jean <fkjean@ccgifortmcmurray.ca>

Brian Jean is out of the country and asked me to answer your letter regarding Marshall Stevenson.

Brian knew Marshall 30 – 40 years ago when he lived as a young boy in Fort McMurray.

Since that time he has had a couple of phone calls from him and an email.

I hope this is the information you require, but Brian cannot verify any information about Marshall.

Mrs. F.K. Jean

1979 Mr.X. makes a complaint to the Canadian Human Rights Commission and later through access to information finds M.J. Hauser of the Correctional Service of Canada in memo(s) also says that Mr.X. was a "murderer" to make sure he remained unemployed!

Instead of verifying this other lie about Mr.X. , the Canadian

Human Rights Commission did nothing about his complaint permitting the RCMP and the Canadian Government to continue their violations to this very day.

1979 Mr.X. makes a complaint to the Canadian Human Rights Commission and later through access to information finds Nicole Bomberg of the Canadian Human Rights Commission in memo(s) also says that Mr.X. was a "murderer" to make sure he remained unemployed.

Instead of verifying this other lie about Mr.X. , the Canadian Human Rights Commission did nothing about his complaint permitting the RCMP and the Canadian Government to continue their violations to this very day.

1979 Mr.X. makes a complaint to the Canadian Human Rights Commission and later through access to information finds Lorisa Stein of the Canadian Human Rights Commission in memo(s) also says that Mr.X. was a "murderer" to make sure he remained unemployed.

Instead of verifying this other lie about Mr.X. , the Canadian Human Rights Commission did nothing about his complaint permitting the RCMP and the Canadian Government to continue their violations to this very day.

1980 Mr.X. being unemployed seeks relief from his Canada Student Loans, however, the Judge turns out to be John Gomery and his request is denied

Mr.X. read with delight that Judge John Gomery was finally revealed as the "biased judge" he was:

A Federal Court ruling has blasted the biased musings of Judge John Gomery
http://www.amazon.com/Federal-ruling-blasted-biased-musings/dp/1456331027/ref=sr_1_4?s=books&ie=UTF8&qid=1393399612&sr=1-4&keywords=%22john+gomery%22
[THIS SUPPRESSED BOOK IS AVAILABLE TO THE CHRC AS A PDF]

1980 Mr.X. being unemployed seeks a disability pension [Canada Pension Plan] using RCMP S/Sgt John Thomas Randle 1979 letter, M.J. Hauser of the Correctional Service of Canada memo(s), Nicole Bomberg of the Canadian Human Rights Commission memo(s) and Lorisa Stein of the Canadian Human Rights Commission memo(s) – his request for disability pension approved [see Appendices below].

1981 Mr.X. being unemployed again seeks relief from his Canada Student Loans, the Judge <u>not</u> being John Gomery, and his request is approved!

1981 The RCMP fabricate more "bull shit" about Mr.X. to railroad him into jail!

1985 Mr.X. re-marries!

Very interesting, the family of the bride received an "anonymous" letter trying to kybosh the wedding?

RCMP S/Sgt John Thomas Randle is well noted for writing letters – did he write this letter too

However, Mr.X. had already revealed the 1976 lies by RCMP S/Sgt John Thomas Randle and his suit against the Canadian Government and the Royal Canadian Mounted Police!

Those that attended the wedding said it was one of the nicest they had ever been to!

An interesting side-piece:

You see, the sister of his brother-in-law's wife married into the Royal Family:

Montrealer Autumn Kelly weds Queen's eldest grandson
Last Updated: Saturday, May 17, 2008

Canadian Autumn Kelly wed the Queen's eldest grandson, Peter Phillips, on Saturday in a ceremony in St. George's Chapel at Windsor Castle attended by about 300 guests, including 70 from Canada.

Kelly grew up in Pointe-Claire, Que., in the largely English-speaking West Island region of Montreal. After attending McGill University [BA majoring in East Asian studies], she worked as a management consultant. She is now employed as a personal assistant to British broadcaster and television personality Michael Parkinson.

Mr.X. also attended McGill University, obtaining a BSW and Management Certificate in Social Services Management.

All of Mr.X. 's in-laws attended the Royal Wedding, meeting the Queen and Prince Philip.

1990 After 14 years of accumulating evidence, Mr. X successfully sues the Canadian Government, the Royal Canadian Mounted Police, the Queen, and RCMP S/Sgt John Thomas Randle over his 1979 letter [see Appendices below].

1990 Mr.X. was hired by the Newfoundland Social Services Department as a Social Worker.

1993 However, Mr.X. would not cover-up the lax security at the Whitbourne Centre run by Newfoundland Social Service Minister Kay Young.

Mr.X. blew the whistle on the lax security at the Whitbourne Centre run by Newfoundland Social Service Minister Kay Young.

Newfoundland Social Service Minister Kay Young and Newfoundland Premier Clyde Wells fabricated statements about Mr.X. to get rid of him for blowing the whistle on the lax security at the Whitbourne Centre!

Newfoundland Social Service Minister Kay Young and Newfoundland Premier Clyde Wells also revealed Mr.X. a PTSD – Chronic Type disability pensioner's name to the media!

Mr.X. Successfully Sued the RCMP: Newfoundland Kay Young reveals PTSD sufferers name to media
[THIS SUPPRESSED BOOK IS AVAILABLE TO THE CHRC AS A PDF]

To make matters worse, because Kay Young and Clyde Wells ignored Mr.X. 's warning, deaths occurred at the Whitbourne Centre:

1995 Death at Newfoundland Social Services Minister Kay Young's Whitbourne Youth Centre
October 8, 1999 (Justice)

1999 Death at Newfoundland Social Services Minister Kay Young's Whitbourne Youth Centre
News Release NLIS 4 March 1, 2001 (Justice)

Attempted Suicide
News Release
NLIS 5; May 29, 2000 (Justice)

Another Attempted Suicide
News Release
NLIS 2; June 29, 2000 (Justice)

Parent concerned about son's treatment
Published on Febuary 14th, 2008
Published on July 2nd, 2010
Barb Sweet, The Telegram

Escape bid foiled at N.L. corrections facility.
Last Updated: Saturday, December 11, 2010
CBC News

N.L. young offenders assault, restrain staff in escape attempt
Published On Sat Dec 11 2010

The Canadian unemployment department could see that Mr.X. had done nothing wrong for blowing the whistle on the lax security at the Whitbourne Centre and approved his application for unemployment benefits!

1995 Mr.X. was offered a Social Work job in Alberta.

However, it appears that Premier Ralph Klein made sure Mr.X. did not take up this position.

Was it a favor to Newfoundland Premier Clyde Wells to keep Mr.X. unemployed?

Was it a favor to the Royal Canadian Mounted Police to keep Mr.X. unemployed?

Mr.X. Successfully Sued the RCMP: Did Ralph Klein help the RCMP to keep the whistleblower unemployed?
[THIS SUPPRESSED BOOK IS AVAILABLE TO THE CHRC AS A PDF]

1996 Being unemployed, Mr.X. went back on his Canada Pension Plan [mental] disability pension with a psychiatrist diagnosis that he suffered with Post Traumatic Stress Disorder – Chronic Type, Social Phobia, etc [see Appendices below].

1990 As part of dealing with his Post Traumatic Stress – Chronic Type Mr.X. took to writing about the RCMP false statements, harassment, illegal, acts:

Human rights violations in Canada: Individual being

denied employment with the Federal Government of Canada due to false "murder charge" statements made by M.J. Hauser of the Correctional Service of Canada (continuing case study from Cour supérieure en matière de faillite, Palais de justice, Montréal, File #500-11-002290-894)OCLC Number: 29205400 – 1990

Human rights violations in Canada: Individual being denied employment with the Federal Government of Canada due to false "murder charge" statements made by Nicole Bomberg of the Public Service Commission of Canada (continuing case study from Cour supérieure en matière de faillite, Palais de justice, Montréal, File #500-11-002290-894)OCLC Number: 29205400 – 1990

1996 As part of dealing with his Post Traumatic Stress – Chronic Type Mr.X. took to writing about the RCMP false statements, harassment, illegal, acts:

R.C.M.P. Sgt. John ("Jack") Thomas Randle's legacy to Canada. ISBN: 0969594429 9780969594420
OCLC Number: 46531882 - 1996

R.C.M.P. Sgt. John ("Jack") Thomas Randle's legacy to Canada. ISBN: 0969594429 9780969594420
OCLC Number: 46531882 - 1996

1997 As part of dealing with his Post Traumatic Stress – Chronic Type Mr.X. took to writing about the RCMP false statements, harassment, illegal, acts:

Human rights violations in Canada by federal agents of the Canadian Human Rights Anti-Discrimination Agency of the Public Service Commission of Canada.
ISBN: 0969594453 9780969594451
OCLC Number: 46528081 - 1997

Is he Canada's example of another Mark Furman : R.C.M.P. Sgt. John ("Jack") Thomas Randle purposefully committed lies, fabricated evidence, made false statements & committed illegal acts! ISBN: 0969594437 9780969594437
OCLC Number: 43152171 - 1997

Complete discharge from bankruptcy including preferred student loans due to Royal Canadian Mounted Police harassment: a most unusual case of bankruptcy.

ISBN: 0968290469 9780968290460
OCLC Number: 46563182 – 1997

1998 As part of dealing with his Post Traumatic Stress – Chronic Type Mr.X. took to writing about the RCMP false statements, harassment, illegal, acts:

Canadian anti-discriminate [sic] directorate and Canadian public service staff Nicole Bomberg's legacy to Canada.
ISBN: 0968290469 9780968290460
OCLC Number: 46563169 - 1998

Canadian anti-discrimination directorate and Canadian public service staff Lorisa Stein's legacy to Canada.
N: 096959447X 9780969594475
OCLC Number: 46563137 - 1998

Royal Canadian Mounted Police officers Sgt. John ("Jack") Thomas Randle's & Cpl. Jackett's legacy to Canada.
ISBN: 0968290442 9780968290446
OCLC Number: 46563215 - 1998

Judge John Gomery's inapproprivate comments based on lies, false statements, fabricated statements & illegal acts by R.C.M.P. Sgt. John Thomas Randle.
ISBN: 0968290477 9780968290477
OCLC Number: 46563154 – 1998

Can police harassment involving illegal acts, false statements and fabricated evidence lead to a diagnosis of post-traumatic stress disorder sufficient to approve permanent disability pension?
ISBN: 0969594488 9780969594482
OCLC Number: 46563102 - 1998

1998 To shut Mr.X. up, the RCMP again fabricated more "bull shit" about Mr.X. in another attempt to railroad him into jail!

2000 The Canadian Investigative Program wasn't interested in Mr.X. :

Story 'too hot' for the investigative program "The Fifth Estate"!!
OCLC Number: 48670944

Likewise, no reply or interest by W - 5, does the conspiracy make sense now?

W-5 Team: Lloyd Robertson, Sandie Rinaldo, Lisa LaFlamme, Victor Malarek and Kevin Newman
W5 (TV series)
The title refers to the Five Ws of journalism: Who, What, Where, When and Why? It is the longest-running newsmagazine/documentary program in North America and the most-watched program of its type in Canada.

2005 How dare Mr.X. move his family back to British Columbia, Canada – a Preponderance of Evidence appears to substantiate that the RCMP would surely make his life miserable, including his wife and children!

Did apparent RCMP conspirator Malaspina University College / Vancouver Island University professor Helen Brown purposefully fabricate a statement about Mr.X. 's son to interfere with his university program

This apparent RCMP conspirator professor Helen Brown also tried the same with Mr.X. 's daughter!

Mr.X. Successfully Sued the RCMP: Malaspina Univ-College teacher Helen Brown lies about missing class
[THIS SUPPRESSED BOOK IS AVAILABLE TO THE CHRC AS A PDF]

How did Malaspina University College / Vancouver Island University reward Helen Brown for her lies about Mr.X. 's children, they made her an Academic Emeritus Designation?

2006 Did the RCMP have the Canadian Military purposefully issue Mr. X's daughter clown sized boots so she would not make BMQ and eliminate her from a career with the Canadian military [see Appendices below]!

And did the doctor, Base Surgeon Major Salsman, treating her purposefully lie to cover the matter up:

Did this military doctor lie: On Purpose
http://www.amazon.com/Did-this-military-doctor-lie/dp/1492770647/ref=sr_1_fkmr0_1?s=books&ie=UTF8&qid=1393401869&sr=1-1-fkmr0&keywords=wallice+bellair+%22the+lying+doctor%22
[THIS SUPPRESSED BOOK IS AVAILABLE TO THE CHRC AS A PDF]

And did Canadian Human Rights Commission agent David Langtry side with the liar Base Surgeon Major Salsman to rule against Mr.X. 's daughter as further RCMP harassment:

David Langtry's Legacy to Canada?: Accepting lie, after lie, after lie?
http://www.amazon.com/David-Langtrys-Legacy-Canada-Accepting/dp/1468160478/ref=sr_1_1?s=books&ie=UTF8&qid=1393409815&sr=1-1&keywords=David+Langtry%E2%80%99s+Legacy+to+Canada%3F
[THIS SUPPRESSED BOOK IS AVAILABLE TO THE CHRC AS A PDF]

2007 Did the RCMP have the Canadian Military apparently "infect" Mr.X. 's son so he would not make BMQ and eliminate him from a career with the Canadian military?

He was sent home with a "mysterious illness" and nothing forthcoming from the Canadian Military nor from Defence Minister Peter MacKay?

Sort of reminds Mr.X. of the poisoning of Warrant Officer Matt Stopford who the Canadian Government "screwed with" until it was too late to save him?

Canadian Government Conspiracy: Was this 'kid' poisoned?
http://www.amazon.com/Canadian-Government-Conspiracy-this-poisoned/dp/146646254X
[THIS SUPPRESSED BOOK IS AVAILABLE TO THE CHRC AS A PDF]

2008 The RCMP apparently had some ruffians harass Mr.X. 's wife, daughter and son

And the Nanaimo RCMP did nothing about it!

Nanaimo RCMP Officer M.R.W. Picard's Legacy to Canada! Threaten the victims?
http://www.amazon.com/Nanaimo-Officer-M-R-W-Picards-Legacy/dp/1467962457/ref=sr_1_38?s=books&ie=UTF8&qid=1323852451&sr=1-38
[THIS SUPPRESSED BOOK IS AVAILABLE TO THE CHRC AS A PDF]

Bar watch shift tonight, I gonna catch me a ginger: What idiot Nanaimo RCMP said this
http://www.amazon.co.uk/watch-shift-tonight-gonna-

ginger/dp/148028923X/ref=sr_1_11?s=books&ie=UTF8&qid=139358407 1&sr=1-11&keywords=does+the+conspiracy+make+sense+now#_
[THIS SUPPRESSED BOOK IS AVAILABLE TO THE CHRC AS A PDF]

2009 Mr.X. moved his family to Winnipeg, Manitoba, Canada to get away from the RCMP harassment in British Columbia, Canada!

However, did the RCMP have a private security employer in Winnipeg, Manitoba, Canada deny Mr.X. 's son essential emails

2009 Did RCMP conspirator Canadian Services Minister Diane Finley purposefully accept lies of a private security employer about Mr.X. 's son to eliminate a career in private security.

Canada's Very Own "Three Blind Mice"! Who concluded that antibiotics are for stress?
http://www.amazon.com/Canadas-Very-Three-Blind-Mice/dp/1466431334/ref=sr_1_3?s=books&ie=UTF8&qid=1393403605&sr=1-3&keywords=Canada%E2%80%99s+Very+Own+%E2%80%9CThree+Blind+Mice%E2%80%9D%21+Who+concluded+that+antibiotics+are+for+stress%3F
[THIS SUPPRESSED BOOK IS AVAILABLE TO THE CHRC AS A PDF]

Canadian Services Minister Diane Finley agent Justice J.M. Bordeleau purposefully accept lies of a private security employer about Mr.X. 's son to eliminate a career in private security.

Liar, Liar, Pants on Fire! J.M. Bordeleau's Legacy to Canada?
http://www.amazon.com/Liar-Pants-Fire-Bordeleaus-Legacy/dp/1468068504/ref=sr_1_43?s=books&ie=UTF8&qid=1323852192&sr=1-43
[THIS SUPPRESSED BOOK IS AVAILABLE TO THE CHRC AS A PDF]

2010 The RCMP made up some cock-and-bull reason not to accept Mr.X. 's son as a recruit thus eliminating his potential career with the RCMP.

The RCMP said Mr.X. 's son had two university degrees and so he was unsuitable?

Mr.X. Successfully Sued the RCMP: [RCMP] Kathleen Gibney says to not hire son because he has two university degrees
[THIS SUPPRESSED BOOK IS AVAILABLE TO THE CHRC AS A PDF]

The RCMP said Mr.X. 's son liked to "catch bad guys" so he was unsuitable?

Mr.X. Successfully Sued the RCMP: [RCMP] Neil Anderson says to not hire son because he likes to catch bad guys, as RCMP payback
[THIS SUPPRESSED BOOK IS AVAILABLE TO THE CHRC AS A PDF]

The RCMP said Mr.X. 's son lived at home so he was unsuitable?

RCMP 'Psychologist' Neil Anderson's Legacy to 'Honesty': Don't tell the applicant our secret?
http://www.amazon.com/RCMP-Psychologist-Andersons-Legacy-Honesty/dp/1467953040/ref=sr_1_37?s=books&ie=UTF8&qid=1322849166&sr=1-37
[THIS SUPPRESSED BOOK IS AVAILABLE TO THE CHRC AS A PDF]

Let's look a little closer at this RCMP 'bull' about Mr.X. 's son?

Instead of hiring a clean-cut recruit like Mr.X. 's son, incredibly the RCMP started hiring drug convicted individuals:

The RCMP, which is on a hiring blitz, will now turn a blind eye to some indiscretions by its applicants, including some drug activities, CBC News has learned.

An internal memo obtained by CBC News reveals the RCMP has changed its policy on drug use "to permit consideration of mitigating factors in all cases of criminal activity, which may include drug trafficking, etc."

Well the reaction to this ridiculous RCMP idea came out good and strong in the "Story Comments" section:

This is such a joke! You can't have criminals being police officers! What are these people on?

I thought the RCMP already hired from the bottom of the barrel? What is left?

Sure, relax the rules and give each new officer 2 tasers. Then they can be twice as dangerous to the public.

I think the standards are too low now. Look at the four liars from Vancouver.

I cannot see how 'lowering the standards' to help in qualifying more candidates for the RCMP is' a step in the right direction'. We should be seeking better quality people for the force, reliable people with a clean background not folks who have committed indiscretions, minor or otherwise. RCMP Officers carry guns, tasers etc. and have a great responsibility to society. We need the very best candidates possible.

RCMP still had some credibility they could find credible applicants. I certainly don't paint all officers with the same brush but the actions of some officers, and how those actions were handled by the institution, have really damaged perceptions of the RCMP. Before looking at lower standards for applicants they should look at higher standards for themselves.

2010 Did apparent RCMP conspirator Manitoba Health Minister Theresa Oswald purposefully accept lies from the "cool kids gang" to harass, isolate and discriminate against Mr.X. 's daughter.

Did RCMP conspirator Manitoba Health Minister Theresa Oswald's "cool kids gang" also try to harass and isolate Mr.X. 's son.

Is there something rotten at Selkirk Mental Health Center: First two female security officers gone after complaining about sex discrimination http://www.amazon.com/something-rotten-Selkirk-Mental-Health/dp/1482090066/ref=sr_1_5?s=books&ie=UTF8&qid=1393404534 &sr=1-5&keywords=wallice+bellair+selkirk
[THIS SUPPRESSED BOOK IS AVAILABLE TO THE CHRC AS A PDF]

2011 As further RCMP harassment Canadian Revenue Minister Gail Shea, knowing full-well that Mr.X. was on a full-disability pension for PTSD – Chronic Type does 5 years of bogus tax audits in 2011, covering the years 2003 to 2009 – the exact years Mr.X. and family had returned to BC before the RCMP harassment got to be too much [see Appendices below].

2012 Canadian Services Minister Diane Finley's staff Joy Sinnott purposely lied so she could deny Mr.X. 's 60 year old wife unemployment benefits:

Mr.X. Successfully Sued the RCMP: Diane Finley denies unemployment application of his wife as RCMP payback
[THIS SUPPRESSED BOOK IS AVAILABLE TO THE CHRC AS A PDF]

Instead, what kind of person does Diane Finley's Department

support in their claim for unemployment benefits – AN ABSOLUTE FRAUDSTER!!!!

Diane Finley's Department cite on "The Index of Jurisprudence - A Supplement to the Digest of Benefit Entitlement Principles – Decision 74065

Claimant was a driver for the employer, who dismissed him because he had used the company's credit card to buy gasoline for his personal automobile. He was filmed at the gas station and a representative of the employer saw the video. The employer wished to press charges against claimant, which was eventually done. The BoR's decision was based on material placed before it; and it did not ignore any material elements. The employers often feel that they have proved claimant's misconduct. However, what they consider bad behaviour sufficient to be cause for dismissal does not necessarily meet the notion of "misconduct" within the meaning of the Act. The employers appeal is dismissed.

WHAT???

Someone commits fraud – yet Diane Finley's Department says not misconduct and approves him for unemployment benefits???

But not Mr.X. 's wife who was following Diane Finley's own Department rules:

29. For the purposes of sections 30 to 33
c. just cause for voluntarily leaving an employment or taking leave from an employment exists if the claimant had no reasonable alternative to leaving or taking leave, having regard to all the circumstances, including any of the following:

ii. obligation to accompany a spouse, common-law partner or dependent child to another residence,

Naturally the book about Diane Finley's behavior was suppressed by Harper and Paulson!!

Diane Finley tries to break up old age married couple
[THIS SUPPRESSED BOOK IS AVAILABLE TO THE CHRC AS A PDF]

2012 To compound Mr.X. 's PTSD - Chronic Type diagnosis and severe Social Phobia a Preponderance of Evidence supports that the Canadian Government [Canadian Prime Minister Stephen Harper] and the RCMP [RCMP Commissioner Robert Paulson] purposely had uploaded the 1976 RCMP / RCMP S/Sgt John Thomas Randle lies that Mr.X. was an "unwilling witness" to the Internet as more harassment and to make sure Mr.X. , his wife and children also remain unemployed and Mr.X. 's PTSD symptoms remained amplified [See Appendices below].

Also, in trying to find someone to do something about these 1976 RCMP / RCMP S/Sgt John Thomas Randle lies to the Internet, Mr.X. wrote to several prominent "legal interested" people, however, Canadian Prime Minister Stephen Harper and RCMP Commissioner Robert Paulson purposely blocked Mr.X. 's email account to these individuals:

Harper blocks email to Professor Warren Magnusson!: Is that legal!
http://www.amazon.com/Harper-blocks-Professor-Warren-Magnusson/dp/1494398028/ref=sr_1_27?s=books&ie=UTF8&qid=1393410154&sr=1-27&keywords=%22Senator+Larry+W.+Campbell%22
[THIS SUPPRESSED BOOK IS AVAILABLE TO THE CHRC AS A PDF]

Harper blocks email to Professor Shannon Sampert!
http://www.amazon.com/Harper-blocks-Professor-Shannon-Sampert/dp/149440995X/ref=sr_1_28?s=books&ie=UTF8&qid=1393410154&sr=1-28&keywords=%22Senator+Larry+W.+Campbell%22
[THIS SUPPRESSED BOOK IS AVAILABLE TO THE CHRC AS A PDF]

Harper blocks email to Professor Lori Turnbull!
http://www.amazon.com/Harper-blocks-email-Professor-Turnbull/dp/1494411822/ref=sr_1_29?s=books&ie=UTF8&qid=1393410154&sr=1-29&keywords=%22Senator+Larry+W.+Campbell%22

Harper blocks emails to 7 Dalhousie University Professors!: Isn't that against the law to interfere with private emails to professors?
http://www.amazon.com/Harper-blocks-Dalhousie-University-Professors/dp/1494421518/ref=sr_1_30?s=books&ie=UTF8&qid=1393410154&sr=1-30&keywords=%22Senator+Larry+W.+Campbell%22
[THIS SUPPRESSED BOOK IS AVAILABLE TO THE CHRC AS A PDF]

Harper blocks emails to 11 University of Ottawa Professors!: Isn't that against the law to interfere with private emails to professors?
http://www.amazon.com/Harper-blocks-emails-University-Professors/dp/1494422123/ref=sr_1_31?s=books&ie=UTF8&qid=1393410154&sr=1-31&keywords=%22Senator+Larry+W.+Campbell%22
[THIS SUPPRESSED BOOK IS AVAILABLE TO THE CHRC AS A PDF]

Mr.X. also wrote to the Chief British Columbia Coroner Lisa Lapointe, without a response from Lisa Lapointe:

Chief Coroner Lisa Lapointe
http://www.amazon.com/Lisa-Lapointe-British-Columbia-Coroner/dp/1482572354/ref=sr_1_1?s=books&ie=UTF8&qid=1393412074&sr=1-1&keywords=Chief+Coroner+Lisa+Lapointe
[THIS SUPPRESSED BOOK IS AVAILABLE TO THE CHRC AS A PDF]

Mr.X. also wrote to the up-and-coming new Prime Minister Justin Trudeau without a response from Justin Trudeau:

Justin Trudeau: What will you do about these illegal acts by PM Harper
http://www.amazon.com/Justin-Trudeau-about-illegal-Harper/dp/1494759365/ref=sr_1_35?s=books&ie=UTF8&qid=1393410154&sr=1-35&keywords=%22Senator+Larry+W.+Campbell%22
[THIS SUPPRESSED BOOK IS AVAILABLE TO THE CHRC AS A PDF]

Mr.X. also wrote to Canadian Supreme Court Justice Beverley McLachlin without a response from Justice Beverley McLachlin:

What will the Supreme Court Justice Beverley McLachlin: Do about this illegal activity by Stephen Harper
http://www.amazon.com/Supreme-Court-Justice-Beverley-McLachlin/dp/1494747480/ref=sr_1_34?s=books&ie=UTF8&qid=1393410154&sr=1-34&keywords=%22Senator+Larry+W.+Campbell%22
[THIS SUPPRESSED BOOK IS AVAILABLE TO THE CHRC AS A PDF]

Mr.X. also made Paul S. Crampton Chief Justice of the Federal Court aware of these events, no reply from him either?

2013 As further RCMP harassment Canadian Revenue Minister Gail Shea, knowing full-well that Mr.X. 's daughter had not lived in British Columbia for years sent her a bogus notice that she owed BC Health money.

Gail Shea: Did Canada Revenue Minister lie
http://www.amazon.com/Gail-Shea-Canada-Revenue-Minister/dp/1482616890/ref=sr_1_50?s=books&ie=UTF8&qid=1393581547&sr=1-50&keywords=wallice+bellair+Stephen+Harper
[THIS SUPPRESSED BOOK IS AVAILABLE TO THE CHRC AS A PDF]

It took some doing but BC finally admitted that Mr.X. 's daughter did not owe BC Health any money!

In addition, as further RCMP harassment in 2014 the new Canadian Revenue Minister Kerry-Lynne D. Findlay [she comes from British Columbia] from tried the same trick on Mr.X. 's son saying he owed BC Health money although the son had not lived in BC for 5 years.

It took some doing but BC finally admitted that Mr.X. 's son did not owe BC Health any money!

In addition, as further RCMP harassment in 2014 the new Canadian Revenue Minister Kerry-Lynne D. Findlay [she comes from British Columbia] also tried the same bogus trick on Mr.X. saying he owed BC Health money although he had not lived in BC for 5 years.

It took some doing but BC finally admitted that Mr.X. did not owe BC Health any money!

2013 Senator Larry W. Campbell, former RCMP officer, and former Chief Coroner says he doesn't care about the 1976 Coroner Inquest results – the RCMP will continue their campaign of illegal acts, harassment of Mr.X. , his wife, and children!!

Mr.X. and Larry Campbell YAWN, Squamish again!
[THIS SUPPRESSED BOOK IS AVAILABLE TO THE CHRC AS A PDF]

When Mr.X. wrote to Senator Larry Campbell about these matters, here's what he had to say:

On 2013-07-02, Larry Campbell sent an email to Mr. X:

The email was from Senator Larry Campbell - <Larry.Campbell@sen.parl.gc.ca>

Senator Larry Campbell, who is a former RCMP officer, wrote –

Yawn

Squamish again

Larry Campbell

Here's the missing and murdered in Squamish, British Columbia, Canada that Senator Larry Campbell, former RCMP officer, doesn't give "two hoots" about:

SQUAMISH # 1

Oct. 29, '85: Rachel Turley, 20
Turley's body was found in a wooded area near Squamish. She had been sexually assaulted, beaten and strangled. Police say she was known to them as a Granville Mall "street person" who once worked as a prostitute.

A 2001 Vancouver Sun article listing the missing
http://www.highwayoftears.ca/missingbclist.htm

SQUAMISH # 2

Topic: 1970's Squamish, BC - possible connection between 3 murders?
Re: 1970's Squamish, BC - possible connection between 3 murders?

« Reply #20 on: August 02, 2011, 04:19:55 PM »

I'm sorry about your friend. Sadly there were so many serial killers in this area during that era, it hard to know for sure.

Unsolved Murders | Missing People Canada
http://www.unsolvedcanada.ca/index.php?topic=3091.15

SQUAMISH # 3

Re: Jodi Henrickson~17~missing~Bowen Island/Squamish~June 20,2009
« Reply #61 on: May 23, 2012, 11:55:54 AM »
Body found on Bowen Island
By Jane Seyd, North Shore News May 23, 2012 6:34 AM

POLICE investigating the discovery of a body in a bushy area of Bowen Island say the remains are likely not those of missing Squamish teen Jodi Henrickson.

"We don't feel it's connected to that case," said Sgt. Jennifer Pound, spokeswoman for the RCMP's Integrated Homicide Investigation Team. Pound said investigators ruled out that the body was Henrickson early on, although she declined to say how police did that.

Bowen Island RCMP were called out Friday at around 2 p.m. by a local resident who had discovered the body on his land, a wooded property in the 1,000 block of Harding Road.

An autopsy is to be performed Tuesday to try to identify the victim and the likely cause of death. Suicide remains a possibility, as does the chance that the body was dumped there.

"There are no obvious signs of injury," said Pound.

So far investigators have not confirmed whether the body - which was badly decomposed - is male or female. "We believe the body was there for quite some time," said Pound.

Lloyd Harding, who lives on Harding Road, said he was walking down to his mailbox with his son's dog at the end of last week when the Jack Russell terrier tried to drag him into the bush.

Harding said he noticed a bad smell in the area. "I thought someone had hit a deer he said."

Harding said he's walked right by the area where the body was found before but didn't see anything or notice any smell in the area before last week's spell of hot weather.

Police are currently checking missing persons reports to see if they can help identify the remains.

Henrickson, then 17, disappeared three years ago on June 20, 2009 after leaving a house party on Bowen Island with her ex-boyfriend Gavin Arnott. Neither Henrickson nor any signs of her have shown up since then, despite several searches by both police and volunteers.

Police have repeatedly said they think Henrickson met with foul play and never left the island.

Harding said the quiet community is "shocked and very concerned" by Friday's discovery.

jseyd@nsnews.com

http://www.nsnews.com/news/Body+found+Bowen+Island/6663655/story.html

Unsolved Murders | Missing People Canada
http://www.unsolvedcanada.ca/index.php?topic=2890.60

SQUAMISH # 4

Christopher Leo Turgeon | 3 | Missing Squamish BC | December 18, 1999
« on: July 17, 2011, 10:39:27 PM »
Case Number: 0000110

Missing Since: 18 December 1999
Missing From: Squamish, British Columbia, CANADA
Details: Christopher was abducted by his non-custodial mother, Lilia VAZQUEZ.
Missing Child:

Christopher Leo TURGEON
Date of Birth: 14 March 1996
Sex: Male
Hair: Brown
Eye: Brown
Height: 91 cm (36 feet, inches)
Weight: 19 kg (42 lb)
Additional Information: He has a mole on his lower lip on the right side. He speaks English and Spanish. Christopher's photo is age-progressed to 7 years old.

May be in the company of:

Lilia Martinez VAZQUEZ
Date of Birth: 23 March 1974
Sex: Female
Hair: Brown
Eye: Brown
Height: 173 cm (68 feet, inches)
Weight: 50 kg (110 lb)
Additional Information: The abductor was born in Mexico. She speaks Spanish and English.
Alias(es): Lilia MARTINEZ, Lilia MARTINEZ VAZQUEZ, Lilia VASQUEZ

Relationship: Mother
http://www.ourmissingchildren.gc.ca/cgi-bin/case.pl?id=181&lang=eng

Unsolved Murders | Missing People Canada
http://www.unsolvedcanada.ca/index.php?topic=5195.0

SQUAMISH # 5

Re: 1950 - 1969 Unsolved Murders and Missing - Canada
« Reply #45 on: April 11, 2010, 06:18:24 PM »

Furry Creek, BC Okay, I am going to post some more of my findings, unfortunately, not much to find. I will post the info over a few posts. This first lot is not in the date sequence as originally listed. I may have found a common thread in these ones. Although they are listed as Squamish/Vancouver cases, when I looked at the death registration information on Ancestry.ca I found all of their locations of death were within 18km of a place called Furry Creek, BC. I have included one that was listed as Squamish as it seems to be in the same area. I am not sure if these young ladies actually died/were found near Furry Creek or if they were perhaps, from there, and therefore, their deaths were listed for that location. I have to break this one into two posts as the computer is fussing

1. 12 April 73 Helen Hopcroft, age 17, Vancouver
Her death was registered as 13 May 73, Furry Creek, BC
There was an obituary for her in the Winnipeg Free Press 7 June 73

2. 17 Feb 75 Gayle Rogers, Vancouver, BC
If it is the same young lady, found "Gail Sandra Rogers" Date of registered death, 7 Mar 75, she was born in 1949 so she was 26, her death is registered as "Squamish, BC"

Unsolved Murders | Missing People Canada
http://www.unsolvedcanada.ca/index.php?topic=416.45

SQUAMISH # 6

Fraser Member
Posts: 120
« Reply #46 on: April 11, 2010, 06:27:30 PM »

Furry Creek cont'd

3. 25 Jan 75 Margie Melinda Blackwell, 21
Death registration: 25 Jan 75, place of death, Furry Creek, BC

4. 26 Feb 76 Ruth Gwendolyn Mallenby, 26, Squamish
Death Registration: "Ruth Gwendelyne Mallenby", 7 Mar 76 Lion's Bay, (18 km from Furry Creek, BC)

For everyone's consideration. If I find anymore with this link I will add them to this post.

Unsolved Murders | Missing People Canada
http://www.unsolvedcanada.ca/index.php?topic=416.45

SQUAMISH # 7

Sunday afternoon a group of hikers found a dead body near a hiking trail on the side of Mamquam Road in Squamish. "It appears the man was met with foul play," said spokeswoman Sgt. Jennifer Pound. "It does appear to be a homicide." Pound also refused to comment on media reports that the man's body was found beaten and duct-taped.

Kim Bolan has reported the identity of the body is that of William Woo from Surrey who was an associate of the East Vancouver hells angels but more recently went over to the other side. Now he's in a body bag. I wonder who the prime suspects are? If the East Vancouver chapter of the Hells angels contract a murder, that makes them a criminal organization guilty of murder. I don't know about the Duhre Daiquiris but Lotus, now there is some old school credibility right there. They are more than capable of professional payback.

Beaten and duck taped. Yeah that would imply foul play. It reminds me of two other cases in Squamish. One was a guy named Alex Larsen who was run over by a truck because he was lying in the middle of the road. It's so strange and tragic. Yes it's possible he got drunk or high and passed out. Yet we've never heard a word either way. We don't know if he was beaten and dumped there or if he was walking on the side of the road and a car hit him which was why he was lying in the middle of the road before the bus ran him over. The case comes to mind and I wish there was more pieces to that puzzle. They say he had made a decision to turn his life around. Just like Britney Irving. Tragic indeed.

Of course there's that other bizarre case in Squamish, the murder of Javan Luke Dowling. Three drug dealers were driving in a car in Vancouver. One of the drug dealers, shot one of the other drug dealers in the head and the third drug dealer watched the shooter cut off Dowling's head and dismembered his body. The two surviving drug dealers buried the body in two separate locations in Squamish. Mihaly Illes was alleged to be the shooter while Derrick Madinski helped him bury the body. Derrick Madinski went with Joe Brallic to LA where Joe was ripped off and murdered.

Meanwhile in that same original article about a new dead body being found in Squamish it later stated there was another shooting in Surrey near the corner of 111A Avenue and 146th Street at about 2: 40 a.m. on Sunday. It didn't even make it's own head line. Kinda sad. The point is violent crime is continuing and as the papers also report the court system is currently in crisis. That was before Harper's disproportionate crime bill sent the fragile system into chaos.

Gangsters Out Blog
http://gangstersout.blogspot.ca/2011/10/body-dumped-in-squamish.html

Senator Larry Campbell ignores 1976 Squamish, B.C. Coroner Inquest Results
http://www.amazon.co.uk/Senator-Campbell-ignores-Squamish-Coroner/dp/1492368873/ref=sr_1_2?s=books&ie=UTF8&qid=1393585222&sr=1-2&keywords=If+you+squeeze+a+%E2%80%9Crat%E2%80%9D+hard+enough
[THIS SUPPRESSED BOOK IS AVAILABLE TO THE CHRC AS A PDF]

2014 Asked RCMP Commissioner Robert Paulson and Privacy Commissioner Chantal Bernier for the return of two letters apparently stolen from Canada Post by that RCMP PSYCHOPATH S/SGT JOHN THOMAS RANDLE with no reply!

2014 CHRC agent Marie Josee Frenette lied in her correspondence to me dated 12 May, 2014 when she said I had never made a Canadian Human Rights Commission complaint [against the RCMP].

As such, is she one of those psychopathic liars Oxford professor Kevin Dutton speaks about?

Canadian human rights commission | Commission canadienne des droits de la personne

Resolution Services Division | Division des services de règlement

MAY 12 2014

PROTECTED

File number: I1400726

Mr.

Dear M

This letter is further to your correspondence of March 20, April 17 and April 20, 2014, addressed to Acting Chief Commissioner David Langtry, and your telephone conversation on April 22, 2014, with Mr. Jamie Masters, Early Resolution Advisor regarding your concerns with a number of federal government departments.

Please note that given his position as Acting Chief Commissioner, it is not appropriate for Acting Chief Commissioner Langtry to respond to correspondence dealing with complaints as he may be called upon to render a decision on a specific file. For this reason, I am responding on his behalf.

Both Mr. Masters and I have reviewed your complaints and related documentation carefully. Unfortunately, they cannot be accepted because they do not meet the requirements of a complaint under the *Canadian Human Rights Act* (CHRA). As such, we have closed your file.

What should I do now?

You can submit new complaint forms if you can fix whatever was missing or unclear in your first complaint form.

What do I need to fix?

. **You have not identified a discriminatory practice outlined in sections 5-14.1 of the Act**

As Mr. Masters informed you in your conversation, on April 22, 2014:

- The Squamish Public Library publishing archived copies of the now-defunct *Squamish Times* newspaper online does not constitute a discriminatory practice under the CHRA.
- There are not reasonable grounds to believe that the online publication of the now-defunct *Squamish Times* newspaper is a move by the RCMP and other government agencies to retaliate against you for an out-of-court settlement you reached with the

.../2

344 Slater Street, Ottawa, Ontario K1A 1E1
344, rue Slater, Ottawa (Ontario) K1A 1E1
Toll-free/Sans frais 1-888-214-1090, TTY/ATS 1-888-643-3304, Fax/Téléc. (613) 996-9661
www.chrc-ccdp.gc.ca

RCMP in the 1990s. In fact, the article from *Pique News Magazine* that you provided in your documentation clearly indicates this was a project undertaken by the Squamish Public Library to continue building its digital archives collection. While you have developed a theory as to how all of the named departments are working in concert against you, on their face these allegations amount to speculation and bald assertions.

- More than speculation is needed to file a complaint. The courts have been clear that "reasonable grounds" require more than just a statement or bald assertion that the conduct is discriminatory. There is an obligation on the part of the complainant to demonstrate that a "reasonable person" in the same circumstances would believe that the policies or practices complained of are discriminatory.

2. You have not shown a link between the alleged discriminatory act(s) and the ground(s) of discrimination.

While you have identified as a person with a disability, you have not made a link between your disability and any of the alleged actions by the PMO, the RCMP, the Copyright Board of Canada, the Privacy Commission of Canada or the Canadian Human Rights Commission. Similarly, you have not made a link to the ground of family status for the complaints you have made on behalf of your family members.

3. A complaint can be no more than three (3) letter-sized pages.

The material you have sent us clearly exceeds the three (3) page limit for a complaint to the Commission. Furthermore, each 3 page complaint must stand on its own. You cannot make reference to attachments and/or previous letters you have sent to the Commission as none of these documents will be sent to the respondents when / if the Commission notifies them of your complaints.

As an aside, it is important that you avoid altering the Commission's complaint kit. Your three (3) page narrative of the complaint must be attached to the complaint kit, not pasted over it.

4. No retaliation as defined in the CHRA

CHRC FALSE STATEMENT

You also allege that the PMO, the RCMP, the Copyright Board of Canada, the Privacy Commission of Canada and the Canadian Human Rights Commission have retaliated against you for the out-of-court settlement you reached with the RCMP in the 1990s. Please note that retaliation in the context of the CHRA refers to situations where a respondent engages in some sort of adverse treatment or threats against a complainant for making a previous CHRC complaint against the same respondent. As you have never filed a formal CHRC complaint against the PMO, the RCMP, the Copyright Board of Canada, the Privacy Commission of Canada or the Canadian Human Rights Commission, by definition none of them could have committed retaliation as outlined in the CHRA.

.../3

344 Slater Street, Ottawa, Ontario K1A 1E1
344, rue Slater, Ottawa (Ontario) K1A 1E1
Toll-free/Sans frais 1-888-214-1090, TTY/ATS 1-888-643-3304, Fax/Téléc. (613) 996-9661
www.chrc-ccdp.gc.ca

Finally, your allegations refer to violations of the *Charter of Rights and Freedoms* and the *Universal Declaration of Human Rights* as well as the CHRA. Please note that the Commission only has the legal authority to deal with complaints under the CHRA. The Commission cannot address alleged violations of the *Charter of Rights and Freedoms* or non-compliance with the *Universal Declaration of Human Rights*.

Given that your complaints are unacceptable in their current form, I am returning the originals and all supporting documents to you and have not kept copies. In addition, I have enclosed some information to assist you should you wish to continue with your complaints. If you have any questions or need more information, please call Mr. Jamie Masters, Early Resolution Advisor at 613-943-9040 or call toll-free at 1-888-214-1090.

Yours sincerely,

Marie Josée Frenette
Early Resolution Team Leader

Encl. Original complaint forms and documentation
Instructions for Filing a Complaint

344 Slater Street, Ottawa, Ontario K1A 1E1
344, rue Slater, Ottawa (Ontario) K1A 1E1
Toll-free/Sans frais 1-888-214-1090, TTY/ATS 1-888-643-3304, Fax/Téléc. (613) 996-9661
www.chrc-ccdp.gc.ca

Appendix A

Did the RCMP have the Canadian Military purposefully issue Mr. X's daughter clown sized boots so she would not make BMQ and eliminate her from a career with the Canadian military!

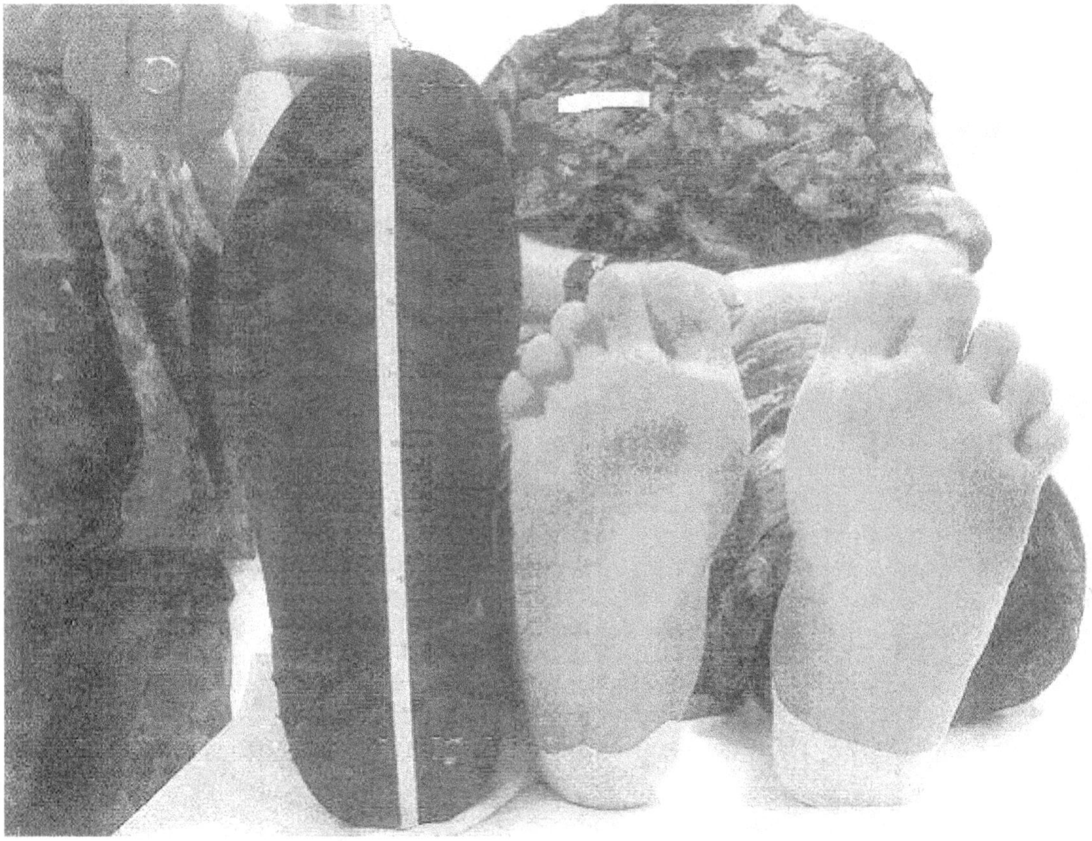

David Langtry, Canadian Human Rights Commission: David Langtry is a Liar Lover http://www.amazon.com/David-Langtry-Canadian-Rights-Commission/dp/1482514753/ref=sr_1_55?s=books&ie=UTF8&qid=1393581547&sr=1-55&keywords=wallice+bellair+Stephen+Harper
[THIS SUPPRESSED BOOK IS AVAILABLE TO THE CHRC AS A PDF]

After all, it had about the lies by RCMP Staff Sgt John Thomas Randle in it!

Canadian Forces Shilo Base Surgeon Major Salsman after recording "blisters and hot spots" on left and right foot – he then lied about the matter in his letter

You can imagine turning up at "boot camp" with these "clown sized" boots and expected to perform tough physical activity!

In any event, Mr.X. 's daughter turned up at "boot camp" in July, 2006.

Surprise, surprise … soon after, on 05 July, 2006 the medical unit at Shilo Manitoba base camp recorded "blisters and hot spots" on left and right foot -- Signed by Canadian Forces Shilo Base Surgeon Major Salsman [See next].

Also recorded in the medical unit at Shilo Manitoba base camp on 05 July, 2006 "on left foot there is a 1" long friction mark on the posterior aspect of the foot slightly proximal from the 'calcaneus(?)'. There is also a blister on the plantar aspect of the foot located on the heel. It appears to be relatively deep. On the right foot there is a similar friction mark as described on the left foot. There are hot spots located on the bottom of both heels" -- Signed by Canadian Forces Shilo Base Surgeon Major Salsman [see next].

As also recorded in the medical unit at Shilo Manitoba base camp on 05 July, 2006 "friction marks, hot spots and blisters caused by grossly oversized combat boots" -- Signed by Canadian Forces Shilo Base Surgeon Major Salsman [see next].

As also recorded in the medical unit at Shilo Manitoba base camp on 05 July, 2006 "enquire about new boots, should be fitted with orthotics, and dressed friction marks, dressed with 'hypafix(?)' and 'mepore(?)' -- Signed by Canadian Forces Shilo Base Surgeon Major Salsman [see next].

The end result, Mr.X. 's daughter was taken from her BMQ course and admitted to Brandon Regional Health Centre on 13 July, 2006 with an infected toe because of the grossly oversized boots she had been issued by my 748 Comm unit "area around blister reddened … pus"!

Finally, as recorded in the medical unit at Shilo Manitoba base camp on 14 July, 2006 it indicated that Mr.X. 's daughter had been "in emergency last night" and then referred to a "blister infected right foot"!

Mr.X. 's daughter was prescribed an antibiotic for her infected foot!

That all seemed straight forward, but then is, until Canadian Forces Shilo Base Surgeon Major Salsman lied about it in his letter dated 17 July, 2006!

In it, Canadian Forces Shilo Base Surgeon Major Salsman who says “I am unsure what is wrong with this lady”!

Another liar!

Signed Major Salsman

000688

DATE	UNIT / UNITÉ	COMPLAINT, EXAMINATION, DIAGNOSIS, TREATMENT, DISPOSAL AND MO'S SIGNATURE / PROBLÈME, EXAMEN, DIAGNOSTIC, TRAITEMENT, ORDONNANCE ET SIGNATURE DU MÉDECIN MILITAIRE
05 July/06 Shilo	ICC	Blisters & on (L) foot and hotspots (L) and (R) feet
	HPI	Yesterday (last night) when she took her boots off, she first noticed blisters right away as well as hotspots. Pain rated 8/10.
	PPM Hx	Pt had blisters 4 mo. ago with her unit when she had even larger boots.
	Meds	Tylenol for headaches see previous entry (4 July/06)
	Allergies	Pollen & Dust
	O/E	On (L) foot there is 1" long friction mark on the posterior aspect of the foot slightly proximal from the calcaneus. There is also a blister on the plantar aspect of the foot, located on the heel. It appears to be ~~quite~~ relatively deep. On the (R) foot there is a similar friction mark as described on the ( ) foot. There are hotspots located on the bottom of both heels
	IMP	Friction marks, ~~and~~ & hotspots and a blister caused by greatly oversized combat boots
	Plan	Enquire about new boots and dressed friction marks. Cpl Lawrence SI RQH Med Tech Scott
		Dressed with hypafix and Mepore. Cpl Lawrence SI RQH Scott
		Should be fitted with orthotics Cpl Lawrence SI RQH Scott
		Concur
		MAJOR KR SALSMAN MD CCFP BSURG 11 CFHSC SHILO 15-684
6 Jul 06	Shilo	19 yr old ♀ c̄ F/u feet ! [illegible]
		[illegible] blister healing well [illegible]

Infected foot - toe

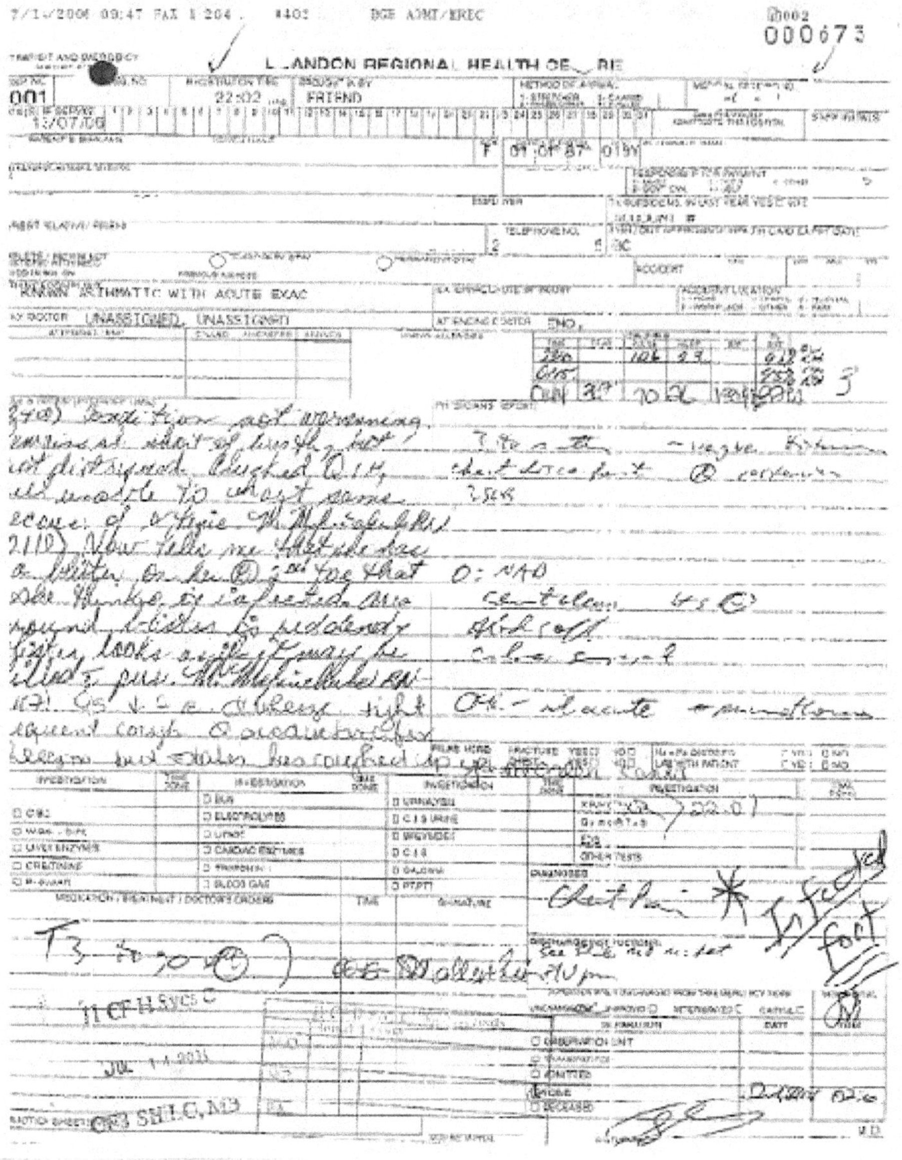

7/1-/2006 09:47 FAX 1 204 . #402 BGE ADMT/EREC

000673

L..ANDON REGIONAL HEALTH CE... RE

001 | 22:02 | FRIEND

13/07/06

F | 01 01 87 | 019Y

KNOWN ASTHMATIC WITH ACUTE EXAC

UNASSIGNED, UNASSIGNED

ENO.

Infected foot

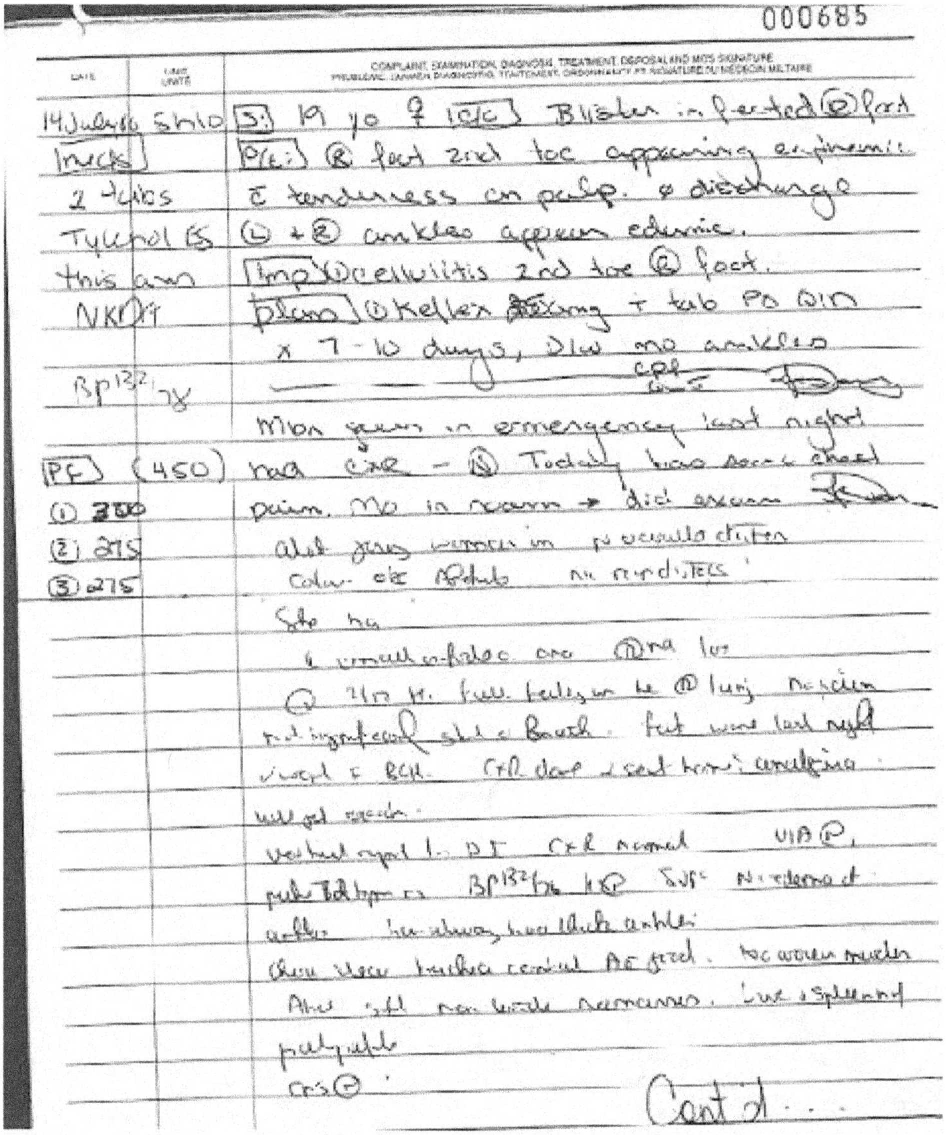

000685

DATE	UNIT / UNITÉ	COMPLAINT, EXAMINATION, DIAGNOSIS, TREATMENT, DISPOSAL AND MO'S SIGNATURE / PROBLÈME, EXAMEN, DIAGNOSTIC, TRAITEMENT, ORDONNANCE ET SIGNATURE DU MÉDECIN MILITAIRE
14 July 06	Shilo	S: 19 yo ♀ [illegible] Blister infected (R) foot
Meds		PE: (R) foot 2nd toe appearing erythematous
2 tabs		c̄ tenderness on palp. ø discharge
Tylenol ES		(L) + (R) ankles appear edematous.
this am		Imp: (1) cellulitis 2nd toe (R) foot.
NKDA		Plan: (1) Keflex [illegible] mg i tab PO QID
		x 7-10 days, D/W MO ankles
BP 132/78		[illegible]
		[illegible] in emergency last night
PF (450)		had CXR - [illegible] Today has [illegible] chest
(1) 300		pain. MO in room → did exam [illegible]
(2) 275		[illegible]
(3) 275		[illegible]
		[illegible]
		[illegible]
		[illegible]
		[illegible]
		[illegible] CXR [illegible]
		[illegible]
		[illegible] CXR normal [illegible]
		[illegible] BP 132/[illegible] [illegible]
		[illegible]
		[illegible]
		[illegible]
		palpable
		CVS (-)
		Cont'd . . .

Antibiotic for infected foot

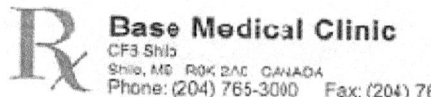

Base Medical Clinic
CFB Shilo
Shilo, MB R0K 2A0 CANADA
Phone: (204) 765-3000 Fax: (204) 765-3303

This Counselling Information was printed for
Rx Number 50359
APO-CEPHALEX 250 MG **DIN: 00768723** Pharm: MP

IMPORTANT NOTE: The following information is intended to supplement, not substitute for, the expertise and judgment of your physician, pharmacist or other healthcare professional. It should not be construed to indicate that use of the drug is safe, appropriate, or effective for you. Consult your healthcare professional before using this drug.

CEPHALEXIN - ORAL (sef-a-LEX-in)

COMMON BRAND NAME(S): Keflex

USES: This medication is a cephalosporin-type antibiotic used to treat a wide variety of bacterial infections (e.g., skin, bone and genitourinary tract infections).

OTHER USES: This drug may also be used before dental procedures in patients with artificial heart valves to prevent serious infection of the heart lining (bacterial endocarditis).

HOW TO USE: Take this medication by mouth usually every 6 or 12 hours, or as directed by your doctor. You may take this medicine with food if stomach upset occurs.

Antibiotics work best when the amount of medicine in your body is kept at a constant level. Therefore, take this drug at evenly spaced intervals.

Continue to take this medication until the full-prescribed amount is finished even if symptoms disappear after a few days. Stopping this medication too early may allow bacteria to continue to grow, which may result in a relapse of the infection.

Inform your doctor if your condition persists or worsens.

SIDE EFFECTS: Stomach upset, headache, fatigue, dizziness, or diarrhea may occur. If any of these effects persist or worsen, notify your doctor or pharmacist promptly.

Tell your doctor immediately if any of these unlikely but serious side effects occur: mental/mood changes.

Tell your doctor immediately if any of these highly unlikely but very serious side effects occur: stomach/abdominal pain, persistent nausea/vomiting, yellowing eyes or skin, dark urine, new signs of infection (e.g., persistent sore throat or fever), easy bruising/bleeding, change in the amount of urine.

This medication may rarely cause a severe intestinal condition (pseudomembranous colitis) due to a resistant bacteria. This condition may occur while receiving therapy or even weeks after treatment has stopped. Do not use anti-diarrhea products or narcotic pain medications if you have the following symptoms because such products may make them worse. Tell your doctor immediately if you develop persistent diarrhea, abdominal or stomach pain/cramping, or blood/mucus in your

---

Formation Health Services
Our Pharmacists will be pleased to answer any questions

Page 1 Produced by Simplicity Plus - Tri-Comp Systems Ltd. Printed on 7/14/2006

724-0144 /2241

Another liar - Canadian Forces Shilo Base Surgeon Major Salsman!

PROTECTED B
National Defence   Défense nationale

11 Canadian Forces Health Services Centre
PO Box 5000 Station Main
Canadian Forces Base Shilo
Shilo MB R0K 2A0

6640-1 (B Surg)

17 July 2006

Adjutant
Communication Reserve School
PO Box 5000 Station Main
Canadian Forces Base Shilo
Shilo MB R0K 2A0

MEDICAL STATUS
PRIVATE

1. I have been asked to provide medical input into this patients condition and use of medical services while on course here. One Medical Officer followed her until he asked me to review her case because he could not find anything wrong.

2. Private , arrived in Shilo on the long weekend in July 2006 and first reported to the MIR on 04 July 2006. There were almost daily (seven visits in 10 days with one weekend) visits for a variety of vague yet disturbing physical complaints. None of which we could find a cause for and mysteriously went away. At one point she asked to stay over night (we have no holding capability). During the stretch of numerous visits she even went to the local Emergency Department. No diagnosis was found then either. Once weekend sick parade started she came to that as well. On the day she did not come, she called the duty medical team to report nefarious symptoms. She was seen again that Monday and still all of her tests were negative as was her exam.

3. I am unsure what is wrong with this lady but I suspect she needs to return to unit and I am quite sure she is unable to tolerate a military environment. She has easily spent more time in my clinic then on her course

4. If further information is required, please do not hesitate to contact the undersigned at local 3150.

K.R. Salsman
Major
Base Surgeon

Appendix 1a

Mr.X. sued for lost wages of 1.3 million dollars [with actuarial evidence] and the first out-of-court settlement that the Federal Government of Canada and the RCMP offered him was $150,000?

The Mr.X. told the lawyer that wasn't enough, and the second out-of-court settlement that the Federal Government of Canada and the RCMP offered him was $275,000?

The Mr.X. said that represented a moral victory over "the bastards" and said accept it!

As far as the Mr.X. is concerned, the Federal Government of Canada and the RCMP still owe him the remaining 1 million dollars, together with a sizeable amount for his wife and children who have themselves been harassed by the Federal Government of Canada and the RCMP!

As far as Mr. X can tell, all he can say is that there are apparently many "lying shit-heads" working for the Federal Government of Canada and the RCMP and that there is enough material out there in the press about them:

Perverts, Sexual Deviants Occupy Top RCMP Ranks – New Allegations Suggest
Saturday, November 12th, 2011
The Link Paper

Appendix 1b **The Mr.X. successfully sued RCMP!**

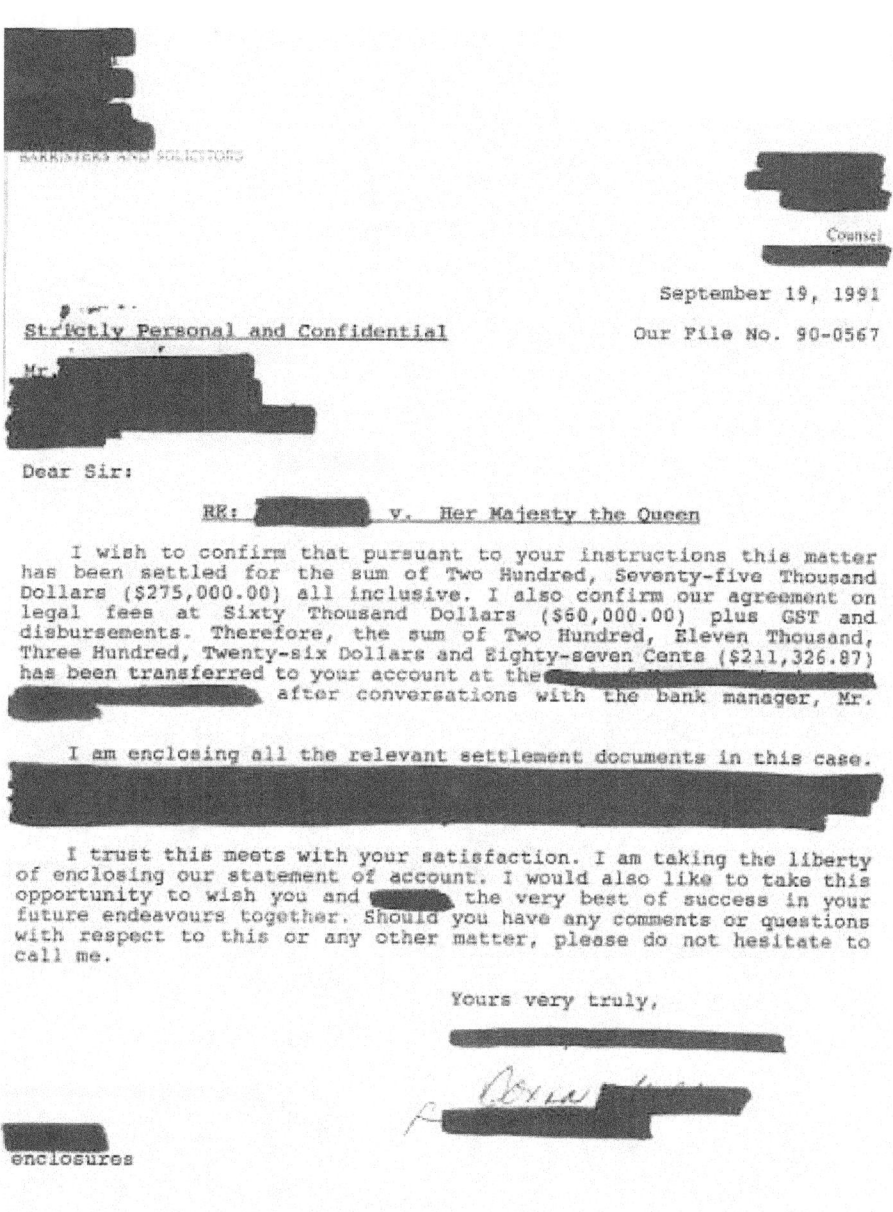

[redacted]
BARRISTERS AND SOLICITORS

[redacted]
Counsel
[redacted]

September 19, 1991

Strictly Personal and Confidential

Our File No. 90-0567

Mr. [redacted]

Dear Sir:

RE: [redacted] v. Her Majesty the Queen

I wish to confirm that pursuant to your instructions this matter has been settled for the sum of Two Hundred, Seventy-five Thousand Dollars ($275,000.00) all inclusive. I also confirm our agreement on legal fees at Sixty Thousand Dollars ($60,000.00) plus GST and disbursements. Therefore, the sum of Two Hundred, Eleven Thousand, Three Hundred, Twenty-six Dollars and Eighty-seven Cents ($211,326.87) has been transferred to your account at the [redacted] after conversations with the bank manager, Mr. [redacted]

I am enclosing all the relevant settlement documents in this case. [redacted]

I trust this meets with your satisfaction. I am taking the liberty of enclosing our statement of account. I would also like to take this opportunity to wish you and [redacted] the very best of success in your future endeavours together. Should you have any comments or questions with respect to this or any other matter, please do not hesitate to call me.

Yours very truly,

[redacted]

[redacted]

[redacted]
enclosures

[redacted] Ottawa, Ontario [redacted] Fax: (613) [redacted] Telephone: (613) [redacted]

Appendix 1c **The Mr.X. successfully sued RCMP!**

16 '9 12:38 JUSTICE CANADA MONTREAL P.3/8

No: T-1131-93

IN THE FEDERAL COURT OF CANADA
TRIAL DIVISION

BETWEEN:

[redacted],

and

Plaintiffs

AND:

HER MAJESTY THE QUEEN, ROYAL CANADIAN MOUNTED POLICE and J.I. RANDLE,

Defendants

DECLARATION OF SETTLEMENT

The parties, by their counsel, hereby declare that the present case has now been settled, each party paying its own costs.

SIGNED in Montreal, this ____ day of September 1991

Appendix 1d **The Mr.X. successfully sued RCMP!**

Minister of Justice
and Attorney General of Canada

Ministre de la Justice
et Procureur générale du Canada

A. Kim Campbell, P.C., Q.C., M.P./c.p., c.r., députée

OCT 15 1991

Mr. David Kilgour, M.P.
House of Commons
Ottawa, K1A 0A6

Dear Mr. Kilgour:

Thank you for your letter of August 21, 1991, concerning Mr. [redacted].

I have been informed that Treasury Board has now approved the proposed settlement and that the cheque is being prepared. The cheque as well as release documents will be forwarded to Mr. [redacted] counsel in the very near future, if this has not already been done.

Yours sincerely,

A. Kim Campbell

RECEIVED - REÇU
OCT 18 1991
HOUSE OF COMMONS
Chambre des Communes

Ottawa, Canada K1A 0H8

Mr.X. went off his Canada Pension Plan disability pension first approved in 1979, thinking the RCMP harassment may have finished?

However, he was unable to cover-up for an apparent "sleeze ball", as Mr. X said!

As cited, Mr. X who lost a job after blowing the whistle on the Whitbourne Centre to Premier Clyde Wells and Social Services Minister Kay Young, had warned these two "idiot" politicians of the dangers at the Whitbourne Centre![1]

However, they wouldn't listen [just like all the Whistelblowers cited in this book and elsewhere[2]] and got rid of their own whistleblower only to find out a year later that a tragedy did occur at the Whitbourne Centre!

With the Newfoundland there was a Whistleblower who wrote to Newfoundland Premier Clyde Wells and to Newfoundland Social Services Minister Kay Young telling them that the security at the maximum security youth centre, the Whitbourne Centre, was lax and should be improved.[3]

What did Newfoundland Premier Clyde Wells and Newfoundland Social Services Minister Kay Young do?

They didn't listen to the Whistleblower; instead they fabricated some cock-and-bull excuse and got rid of him, just like all the government ministers and managers cited in this book and elsewhere.[4]

And what did that "sleaze-ball" Social Services Minister Kay Young do; she even violated the violation of the Freedom of Information Act and the Privacy Act to make sure this whistleblowers was good-and-gone!

Can't have anyone blowing the whistle on political / government incompetence can we:

November 16, 1994
HOUSE OF ASSEMBLY PROCEEDINGS
Vol. XLII No. 62
http://www.assembly.nl.ca/business/hansard/ga42session2/94-11-16.htm

MR. FITZGERALD: Thank you, Mr. Speaker.

My question is to the Minister of Social Services. I want to ask the Minister of Social Services why she released information on the employment history of a Mr. xx, the former operations manager at the Newfoundland and Labrador Youth Centre, in clear violation of the Freedom of Information Act and in violation I believe of the Privacy Act?

MR. FITZGERALD: Mr. Speaker, not only did the minister violate the Freedom of Information and Privacy Act but she also gave false information, Mr. Speaker, about Mr. xx's employment history. The minister said that Mr. xx had been fired for reasons related to job performance. The official record of employment the department gave to Mr. xx and to Employment Canada says he was dismissed for breach of trust and loss of confidence. Now I ask the minister, did the minister know, Mr. Speaker, that she was giving false information in her press release? Will she now admit Mr. xx was fired because he blew the whistle and disclosed the information as to what was actually happening out at the Newfoundland and Labrador Youth Centre?

Now comes that "sleaze-ball" Newfoundland Premier Clyde Wells:

November 17, 1994
HOUSE OF ASSEMBLY PROCEEDINGS
Vol. XLII No. 63
http://www.assembly.nl.ca/business/hansard/ga42session2/94-11-17.htm

MR. W. MATTHEWS: Thank you very much, Mr. Speaker.

I have a question for the Premier, following up on the line of questioning by the member for Bonavista South yesterday dealing with the Minister of Social Services Kay Young. Now, on November 8, 1994 the Minister of Social Services Kay Young issued a public statement, a written press release, where she referred to the dismissal of one Mr. xx at the Newfoundland and Labrador Youth Center at Whitbourne. In that she talked about the reasons for dismissal, job performance and work history.

I want to ask the Premier, in light of the minister's public statement that is clearly a violation of the Freedom of Information Act and the Privacy Act, but particularly the Freedom Information Act, section 10 (1) (b): Does the Premier consider this conduct and behavior of the Minister of Social Services Kay Young to be acceptable?

MR. W. MATTHEWS: - and in that written, deliberate statement pertaining to the situation, she said: Mr. xx was dismissed for work related problems, job performance. Now the record of employment belonging to Mr. xx states that he was dismissed for breach of trust and loss of confidence, so in essence, the minister in her statement, issued a false statement. The reason was inaccurate and incorrect, so I want to ask the Premier: does he feel that the conduct of the Minister of Social Services

Kay Young, in issuing a false, public statement is behaviour and conduct acceptable for a minister of his Administration or, is he going to allow the standards and behaviour and conduct of the ministers to sink to an all-time low in this Province, where, individual privacy will no longer be protected?

What happened a year later, due to the lax security, one of the youth committed suicide and a stink was raised about Newfoundland Premier Clyde Wells and Newfoundland Social Services Minister Kay Young ignoring these Whistleblower warnings!

Footnotes

1. *The Newfoundland Department of Social Services is the worst department this author has ever read about*, AMICUS No. 16972196, National Library of Canada.

2. *Some Canadian Whistleblowers*
Topics: Whistleblowers
http://fairwhistleblower.ca/wbers/canadian_wbs.html

3. *The Newfoundland Department of Social Services is the worst department this author has ever read about*, AMICUS No. 16972196, National Library of Canada.

4. *Some Canadian Whistleblowers*
Topics: Whistleblowers
http://fairwhistleblower.ca/wbers/canadian_wbs.html

To make matters worse, because these two ignored Mr. X's warning, deaths occurred at the Whitbourne Centre:

> *1995 Death at Newfoundland Social Services Minister Kay Young's Whitbourne Youth Centre*
> October 8, 1999 (Justice)
>
> *1999 Death at Newfoundland Social Services Minister Kay Young's Whitbourne Youth Centre*
> News Release NLIS 4 March 1, 2001 (Justice)
>
> *Attempted Suicide*
> News Release
> NLIS 5; May 29, 2000 (Justice)
>
> *Another Attempted Suicide*
> News Release

NLIS 2; June 29, 2000 (Justice)

Parent concerned about son's treatment
Published on Febuary 14th, 2008
Published on July 2nd, 2010
Barb Sweet, The Telegram

Escape bid foiled at N.L. corrections facility.
Last Updated: Saturday, December 11, 2010
CBC News

N.L. young offenders assault, restrain staff in escape attempt
Published On Sat Dec 11 2010

Appendix 3b

Mr.X. was diagnosed with a multitude of disorders as a consequence of RCMP and Federal Government illegal acts, harassment and other abuse.

Author's note: Anyone who has to identify a loved-one in the morgue can appreciate the horror, grief, anger one experiences?

September 24th, 1996

The Medical Advisor
Income Security Programs
333 River Rd
Ottawa, Ontario
K1A 9Z9

OCT 7 1996

Dear Sir or Madame:

Re:

I am writing a letter on behalf of one of my patients who suffers from a grievous mental malady. He has been previously accepted for CPP disability.

His case is complicated. He is a very accomplished gentleman who has two advanced degrees including a Ph.D. and yet cannot work. He spends his time largely sequestered at home writing notes and letters and suffers extreme anxiety if he attempts to go outside.

He is very secretive about events that happened in the past but evidently he sustained a major personal loss in 1976 and ever since then has never recovered. He has paranoid ideas and symptoms of marked anxiety. I have been treating him as best I could as a family physician but felt his symptoms were aggravated and complicated enough that I referred him to a psychiatrist.

suffers from many symptoms of post-traumatic stress disorder and unresolved grief.....fear, guilt, horror, dreams of traumatic content, social avoidancy, decreased interest, impaired memory, irritability, anger, increased vigilance, sense of futility regarding the future, some paranoid ideations.

Appendix 3c

Mr.X. was diagnosed with a multitude of disorders as a consequence of RCMP and Federal Government illegal acts, harassment and other abuse.

Anyone who has to identify a loved-one in the morgue can appreciate the horror, grief, anger one experiences?

October 17, 1996

FRANCOISE LeBLANC, R.N., B.A.,
DISABILITY OPERATIONS DIVISION
333 RIVER ROAD
OTTAWA, CANADA K1A 0L1

RE:

Dear Francoise,

Thank you for your letter of October 1, 1996

gives a 20 year history of Post-Traumatic Stress Disorder following the homicide of a colleague in a prison uprising and also the murder in 1976. I believe you are well aware of these events and that was falsely accused of the latter crime. The effect on his family relationships and on him are also well documented. has become very suspicious of others especially Government agencies and is somewhat paranoid. This paranoia has made it difficult for him to accept psychological help as a degree of trust is almost essential. He seems to have made numerous attempts to improve his occupational situation, but his difficulties dealing with others always overwhelm him.

When seen, exhibited and described numerous signs and symptoms of Post-Traumatic Stress Disorder including marked agitation whenever the subject of the murder loomed. He described fear, guilt and horror, traumatic dreams, social avoidance, loss of interest, poor memory for details of the murder, irritability, anger, increased vigilance, a sense of futility re. the future, difficulties with emotional involvement, and arousal by recollections of the trauma including those precipitated by news stories of similar events. In interviews, he is often tearful ,distraught and agitated.

Diagnostically, he has 1) Post-Traumatic Stress Disorder -Chronic Type
2) Social Phobia -secondary to 1)

Appendix 3d

Mr.X. was diagnosed with a multitude of disorders as a consequence of RCMP and Federal Government illegal acts, harassment and other abuse.

April 1, 1998

To: Mr. Denis Duhamel
Tower A, 11th floor
Place Vanier

From: Dr. N. Kanjilal
Medical Advisor

Subject:

As per your request, I reviewed the file of to determine the basis for granting him the disability benefits.

You are well aware that we are guided by the CPP Legislation which states that a person must be suffering from a physical and/or mental disability which is both severe and prolonged to be eligible to receive disability benefits. Severe means that the person must be incapable of pursuing any substantially gainful occupation regularly. Prolonged means that the incapacity to work at any substantially gainful occupation will likely be long continued and of indefinite duration. To assess such disability we have to ascertain the limiting loss or absence of the capacity to meet the occupational demands according to the regulatory requirements described above.

seems to have satisfied the legislation and in our judgement he is incapable to carry out any occupational demands.

will be well advised to consult his treating physicians if he wishes to find out about any particular medical condition, who will be in a better position to explain his specific question.

Hope this answers some of your problems. Please do not hesitate to contact me should you need any other information.

Dr. N. Kanjilal
Tel: 952-3620

RCMP commissioner Bob Paulson 'truly sorry' for perceived slight against mentally ill

Douglas Quan, Postmedia News, June 18, 2013

The RCMP commissioner says he is "truly sorry" for making a sound and gesture during a town hall earlier this year that some have interpreted as a slight against people suffering from mental-health issues.

The website that posted the audio clip, re-sergeance.net, suggested that as Paulson whistled, he also twirled his finger by the side of his head.

Mr.X. has the original Coroner Inquest report sent to him by the Coroner's office of British Columbia Canada and the Coroner personally apologized to Mr.X. for listening to the lies by the RCMP / RCMP Staff Sgt John Thomas Randle!!

Province of
British Columbia

Solicitor General

March 1, 1989

Mr.
C.P. 2181
Dorval, P.Q.
H9S 3K9

Dear Mr.

SUBJECT: <u>Coroner's Inquest</u>

As per your written request please find attached a certified true copy of the transcript from the Inquest into the unfortunate death of . I trust this transcript will provide you with the information that you require.

Yours truly,

Debi Rupert
Secretary

/dr
Attachment

P. 3①⓪

The letters and numbers [P3ai] at the bottom of the above noted letter refers to the evidence the Mr.X. submitted to the Federal Court of Canada when he SUCCESSFULLY SUED the Royal Canadian Mounted Police and the Federal Government of Canada!!

The RCMP didn't like this and has harassed Mr. X, his wife and children since that time!!!

DEFENCE First of all in respect to the arrangements and the arrest of this man, he was not represented by counsel on any of the submissions and I would have respectfully would have desired an opportunity to have made that representation for him in respect to that warrant, that was issued

in respect to this matter. Secondly, I was completely unaware of the arrest.' I was at a location where a phone was not available readily, and I was not aware of the fact that this matter of the arrest had come on. It was not a question of arranging at my convenience, it was a matter of him appearing in my absence, and that knowledge that I was going to be absent for awhile was information that the Crown had.

DEFENCE

Mr. Coroner, there is one point I feel I must raise before the jury are excused. I wish to stress that I have reviewed the transcript of the proceedings of the last occasion we were here, and I was disturbed in the extreme to read of the comments made on the voluntariness of my client and I feel that no prejudicial leanings should be taken from that. My client was not notified or asked to appear.

The verdict in this 1976 Coroner's Inquest – by persons or persons unknown:

.ERDICT 149

REMARKS 148
Inquest.)

CORONER

Has the jury reached a verdict?

We find that this death was unnatural and that it was homicide. We find that some person or persons unknown are to blame. We recommend that investigation be continued.

CORONER Do you all so find?

JURORS We do.

CORONER Thank you gentlemen and ladies for your attendance her to-night.

L. C. KINDREE, M.D.,
Coroner

I hereby certify the foregoing to be a true and accurate transcript of the proceedings herein to the best of my skill and ability.

Evelyn A. McCartney,
Official Court Reporter.

The RCMP put some bull-shit about the Mr.X. – this time that he was an unwilling witness which is what the RCMP / RCMP Staff Sgt John Thomas Randle [through the Crown] told the Coroner in 1976 causing Mr.X. to miss his wife's funeral!!!

DEFENCE

First of all in respect to the arrangements and the arrest of this man, he was not represented by counsel on any of the submissions and I would have respectfully would have desired an opportunity to have made that representation for him in respect to that warrant, that was issued

in respect to this matter. Secondly, I was completely unaware of the arrest.' I was at a location where a phone was not available readily, and I was not aware of the fact that this matter of the arrest had come on. It was not a question of arranging at my convenience, it was a matter of him appearing in my absence, and that knowledge that I was going to be absent for awhile was information that the Crown had.

DEFENCE

Mr. Coroner, there is one point I feel I must raise before the jury are excused. I wish to stress that I have reviewed the transcript of the proceedings of the last occasion we were here, and I was disturbed in the extreme to read of the comments made on the voluntariness of my client and I feel that no prejudicial leanings should be taken from that. My client was not notified or asked to appear.

Appendix D

As further RCMP harassment Canadian Revenue Minister Gail Shea, knowing full-well that Mr.X. was on a full-disability pension for PTSD – Chronic Type does 5 years of bogus tax audits in 2011, covering the years 2003 to 2009 – the exact years Mr.X. and family had returned to BC!

Canadian Revenue Minister Gail Shea joins RCMP, and does bogus audits of Mr.X. , as further harassment and RCMP payback for successfully suing them?

Bogus audit 2003 instigated by RCMP

Canada Revenue Agency — Agence du revenu du Canada

NOTICE OF REASSESSMENT

1

Date	Name	Social insurance no.	Tax year	Tax centre
Jan 11, 2011			2003	

At a later date, we may review your return to verify income you reported or deductions and credits you claimed. Keep all your slips, receipts, and other supporting documents in case we ask to see them.

Explanation of changes and other important information

This notice explains the results of our reassessment of your income tax return and any changes we may have made. Please refer to the "Summary" area for additional information.

We have adjusted your return to update your tuition and education amounts for carryforward.

We are mailing to you separately your reassessment notices for two or more taxation years. The notice for the latest taxation year will show your combined total refund or balance due. We will send you any refund to which you are entitled after we have reassessed all your returns.

According to this reassessment, you have unused federal and Ontario tuition and education amounts of $1,600 and $1,662, respectively, that you can carry forward to a future year.

If you have any questions about your reassessment, please call our Enquiries service at 1-800-959-8281. If you need to contact another area of the Agency, see the telephone listings in the government section of your telephone book.

Canadian Revenue Minister Gail Shea joins RCMP, and does bogus audits of Mr.X. , as further harassment and RCMP payback for successfully suing them?

Bogus audit 2004 instigated by RCMP

Canada Revenue Agency | Agence du revenu du Canada

NOTICE OF REASSESSMENT

1

Date	Name	Social insurance no.	Tax year	Tax centre
Jan 11, 2011			2004	

At a later date, we may review your return to verify income you reported or deductions and credits you claimed. Keep all your slips, receipts, and other supporting documents in case we ask to see them.

Explanation of changes and other important information

This notice explains the results of our reassessment of your income tax return and any changes we may have made. Please refer to the "Summary" area for additional information.

We have adjusted your return to update your tuition and education amounts for carryforward.

We are mailing to you separately your reassessment notices for two or more taxation years. The notice for the latest taxation year will show your combined total refund or balance due. We will send you any refund to which you are entitled after we have reassessed all your returns.

According to our records, you have unused federal and British Columbia tuition and education amounts of $1,600 and $1,600, respectively, that you can carry forward to a future year.

If you have any questions about your reassessment, please call our Enquiries service at 1-800-959-8281. If you need to contact another area of the Agency, see the telephone listings in the government section of your telephone book.

Canadian Revenue Minister Gail Shea joins RCMP, and does bogus audits of Mr.X. , as further harassment and RCMP payback for successfully suing them?

Bogus audit 2005 instigated by RCMP

Canada Revenue Agency | Agence du revenu du Canada

NOTICE OF REASSESSMENT

1

Date	Name	Social insurance no.	Tax year	Tax centre
Jan 11, 2011			2005	

At a later date, we may review your return to verify income you reported or deductions and credits you claimed. Keep all your slips, receipts, and other supporting documents in case we ask to see them.

Explanation of changes and other important information

This notice explains the results of our reassessment of your income tax return and any changes we may have made. Please refer to the "Summary" area for additional information.

We have adjusted your return to update your tuition and education amounts for carryforward.

We are mailing to you separately your reassessment notices for two or more taxation years. The notice for the latest taxation year will show your combined total refund or balance due. We will send you any refund to which you are entitled after we have reassessed all your returns.

According to our records, you have unused federal and British Columbia tuition and education amounts of $1,600 and $1,600, respectively, that you can carry forward to a future year.

If you have any questions about your reassessment, please call our Enquiries service at 1-800-959-8281. If you need to contact another area of the Agency, see the telephone listings in the government section of your telephone book.

Canadian Revenue Minister Gail Shea joins RCMP, and does bogus audits of Mr.X. , as further harassment and RCMP payback for successfully suing them?

Bogus audit 2006 instigated by RCMP

Canada Revenue Agency | Agence du revenu du Canada

NOTICE OF REASSESSMENT

Date	Name	Social insurance no.	Tax year	Tax centre
Jan 11, 2011			2006	

At a later date, we may review your return to verify income you reported or deductions and credits you claimed. Keep all your slips, receipts, and other supporting documents in case we ask to see them.

Explanation of changes and other important information

This notice explains the results of our reassessment of your income tax return and any changes we may have made. Please refer to the "Summary" area for additional information.

We have adjusted your return to update your tuition and education amounts for carryforward.

According to our records, you have unused federal tuition, education, and textbook amounts of $1,600 that you can carry forward to a future year.

According to our records, you have unused British Columbia tuition and education amounts of $1,600 that you can carry forward to a future year.

We are mailing to you separately your reassessment notices for two or more taxation years. The notice for the latest taxation year will show your combined total refund or balance due. We will send you any refund to which you are entitled after we have reassessed all your returns.

If you have any questions about your reassessment, please call our Enquiries service at 1-800-959-8281. If you need to contact another area of the Agency, see the telephone listings in the government section of your telephone book.

Canadian Revenue Minister Gail Shea joins RCMP, and does bogus audits of Mr.X. , as further harassment and RCMP payback for successfully suing them?

Bogus audit 2007 instigated by RCMP

Canada Revenue Agency | Agence du revenu du Canada

NOTICE OF REASSESSMENT

1

Date	Name	Social insurance no.	Tax year	Tax centre
Jan 11, 2011			2007	

At a later date, we may review your return to verify income you reported or deductions and credits you claimed. Keep all your slips, receipts, and other supporting documents in case we ask to see them.

Explanation of changes and other important information

This notice explains the results of our reassessment of your income tax return and any changes we may have made. Please refer to the "Summary" area for additional information.

We have adjusted your return to update your tuition and education amounts for carryforward.

According to our records, you have unused federal tuition, education, and textbook amounts of $1,600 that you can carry forward to a future year.

According to our records, you have unused British Columbia tuition and education amounts of $1,600 that you can carry forward to a future year.

We are mailing to you separately your reassessment notices for two or more taxation years. The notice for the latest taxation year will show your combined total refund or balance due. We will send you any refund to which you are entitled after we have reassessed all your returns.

If you have any questions about your reassessment, please call our Enquiries service at 1-800-959-8281. If you need to contact another area of the Agency, see the telephone listings in the government section of your telephone book.

Canadian Revenue Minister Gail Shea joins RCMP, and does bogus audits of Mr.X. , as further harassment and RCMP payback for successfully suing them?

Bogus audit 2008 instigated by RCMP

Canada Revenue Agency — Agence du revenu du Canada

NOTICE OF REASSESSMENT

Date: Jan 11, 2011

Tax year: 2008

At a later date, we may review your return to verify income you reported or deductions and credits you claimed. Keep all your slips, receipts, and other supporting documents in case we ask to see them.

Explanation of changes and other important information

This notice explains the results of our reassessment of your income tax return and any changes we may have made. Please refer to the "Summary" area for additional information.

We have adjusted your return to update your tuition and education amounts for carryforward.

According to our records, you have unused federal tuition, education, and textbook amounts of $1,600 that you can carry forward to a future year.

According to our records, you have unused British Columbia tuition and education amounts of $1,600 that you can carry forward to a future year.

We are mailing to you separately your reassessment notices for two or more taxation years. The notice for the latest taxation year will show your combined total refund or balance due. We will send you any refund to which you are entitled after we have reassessed all your returns.

If you have any questions about your reassessment, please call our Enquiries service at 1-800-959-8281. If you need to contact another area of the Agency, see the telephone listings in the government section of your telephone book.

Canadian Revenue Minister Gail Shea joins RCMP, and does bogus audits of Mr.X. , as further harassment and RCMP payback for successfully suing them?

Bogus audit 2009 instigated by RCMP

Canada Revenue Agency / Agence du revenu du Canada

NOTICE OF REASSESSMENT

Date: Jan 11, 2011

Tax year: 2009

At a later date, we may review your return to verify income you reported or deductions and credits you claimed. Keep all your slips, receipts, and other supporting documents in case we ask to see them.

Explanation of changes and other important information

This notice explains the results of our reassessment of your income tax return and any changes we may have made. Please refer to the "Summary" area for additional information.

We have adjusted your return to change the province of residence to Manitoba.

According to our records, you have unused federal tuition, education, and textbook amounts of $1,600 that you can carry forward to a future year.

According to our records, you have unused British Columbia tuition and education amounts of $1,600 that you can carry forward to a future year.

Based on available information at the beginning of 2011, your unused Tax-Free Savings Account (TFSA) contribution room is $15,000. For detailed information, visit My Account on our website at www.cra.gc.ca/myaccount. If you become a non-resident of Canada and later make a contribution to a TFSA, you may have to pay a tax. For more information, visit our website at www.cra.gc.ca/tfsa.

If you have any questions about your reassessment, please call our Enquiries service at 1-800-959-8281. If you need to contact another area of the Agency, see the telephone listings in the government section of your telephone book.

Appendix E

As further RCMP harassment Canadian Revenue Minister Gail Shea, knowing full-well that Mr.X. 's daughter had not lived in British Columbia for years sent her a bogus notice that she owed BC Health Money!

Another "scam" by Canadian Revenue Minister Gail Shea saying daughter owed money to BC Health – it took some doing but this was a lie!

Government of Canada Gouvernement du Canada

ST JOHNS NL A1B 3Z1

004349

Account: 003602145174

January 18, 2013

Dear F

According to our records, you have an outstanding debt under the following legislation or program:

Name of Act or Program: Medical Services Plan Premiums
Name of Department: Revenue Services of British Columbia
Jurisdiction: British Columbia

We would like to inform you that section 164(2) of the Income Tax Act allows the Canada Revenue Agency to apply any income tax refund or certain tax credits otherwise payable to you against certain outstanding federal, provincial, or territorial government debts you owe.

HP Advanced Solutions Inc., operating under the name Revenue Services of British Columbia, provides collection services on behalf of the Province of British Columbia. Please contact Revenue Services of British Columbia to discuss or settle this debt. They can assist you with the resolution of your debt by providing you with more information and letting you know about payment options.

You can call Revenue Services of British Columbia toll free at 1-877-405-4965 from Monday to Thursday between 8:00 a.m. and 7:00 p.m. (PT), Friday between 8:00 a.m. and 4:30 p.m. (PT), and Saturday between 10:00 a.m. and 4:00 p.m. (PT). You can also reach them:

- by mail at P.O. Box 9401 Stn Prov Govt Victoria BC V8W 9S6; or
- by fax at 1-250-405-4412 or 1-250-405-4410

You can also find information online at: http://www.sbr.gov.bc.ca/individual.html

Canada Revenue Agency
On Behalf of: Revenue Services of British Columbia

Appendix F

It took some doing but BC finally admitted that Mr.X. 's daughter did not owe BC Health any money!

Another "scam" by Canadian Revenue Minister Gail Shea saying daughter owed money to BC Health – it took some doing but this was a lie!

BRITISH COLUMBIA | Health InsuranceBC

Account 25178575

February 18, 2013

Dear

Your father's email to the Minister of Health has been referred to our office as Health Insurance BC is responsible for the administration of the Medical Services Plan and PharmaCare benefits.

Our records show that you were receiving Medical Services Plan (MSP) coverage as a dependent on your father's coverage until you turned 25 years of age (January 31, 2012) as our office was informed you were in full-time attendance at school/university.

When a child is no longer eligible for coverage as a dependent under their parent's plan, separate coverage is established for the child. Premium free coverage is provided until the following June 30th, by which time the child should have completed an application for premium assistance to determine his/her eligibility for premium assistance. An application for premium assistance is mailed to the child during spring of the year in which his/her premium-free coverage will end.

A separate account was established for you effective February 1, 2012 and an application for premium assistance was mailed to you at the most recent address on file for you while you were covered on your father's plan. When a signed application for premium assistance was not received from you, your premium rate was adjusted to the full rate effective July 1, 2012. MSP premium invoices were sent to the same address, 13-855 Howard Ave, Nanaimo, B.C. V9R 5V4.

Now that we have been informed that you have not resided in British Columbia since 2009, your MSP coverage has been cancelled. Since the exact date of your move outside British Columbia has not been provided, your coverage has been cancelled retroactive to December 31, 2009. There are no MSP premiums outstanding on your account.

I trust this clarifies the standing of your account.

Yours truly,

S. Krieger
Administrative Review Officer

Health Insurance BC
www.hibc.gov.bc.ca

PO Box 9035 Stn Prov Govt
Victoria BC V8W 9E3

Lower Mainland: 604 683-7151
Rest of BC: 1 800-663-7100

Appendix G

In addition, as further RCMP harassment in 2014 the new Canadian Revenue Minister Kerry-Lynne D. Findlay tried the same bogus trick on Mr.X. 's son saying he owed BC Health money although the son had not lived in BC for 5 years!

It took some doing but BC finally admitted that Mr.X. 's son did not owe BC Health any money!

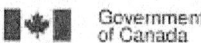

Government of Canada Gouvernement du Canada

ST. JOHN'S NL A1B 3Z1

Account: 003602145144

January 8, 2014

Dear

According to our records, you have an outstanding debt under the following legislation or program:

Name of Act or Program: Medical Services Plan Premiums
Name of Department: Revenue Services of British Columbia
Jurisdiction: British Columbia

We would like to inform you that section 164(2) of the Income Tax Act allows the Canada Revenue Agency to apply any income tax refund or certain tax credits otherwise payable to you against certain outstanding federal, provincial, or territorial government debts you owe.

HP Advanced Solutions Inc., operating under the name Revenue Services of British Columbia, provides collection services on behalf of the Province of British Columbia. Please contact Revenue Services of British Columbia to discuss or settle this debt. They can assist you with the resolution of your debt by providing you with more information and letting you know about payment options.

You can call Revenue Services of British Columbia toll free at 1-877-405-4965 from Monday to Thursday between 8:00 a.m. and 7:00 p.m. (PT), Friday between 8:00 a.m. and 4:30 p.m. (PT), and Saturday between 10:00 a.m. and 4:00 p.m. (PT). You can also reach them:
- by mail at P.O. Box 9401 Stn Prov Govt Victoria BC V8W 9S6; or
- by fax at 1-250-405-4412 or 1-250-405-4410

You can also find information online at: http://www.sbr.gov.bc.ca/individual.html

Canada Revenue Agency
On Behalf of: Revenue Services of British Columbia

Appendix H

In addition, as further RCMP harassment in 2014 the new Canadian Revenue Minister Kerry-Lynne D. Findlay also tried the same bogus trick on Mr.X. son saying he owed BC Health money although he had not lived in BC for 5 years [see Appendix H below]!

It took some doing but BC finally admitted that Mr.X. did not owe BC Health any money!

BRITISH COLUMBIA | Health InsuranceBC

Account 28863215

February 3, 2014

Within Canada
When a resident of Canada enrolled with MSP leaves British Columbia to reside elsewhere in Canada, benefits are provided for the balance of the month of departure plus two months. If requested, benefits may be extended up to three extra months to cover you while in transit.

Outside Canada
When a resident enrolled with MSP leaves British Columbia to reside outside Canada, benefits are provided for the balance of the month of departure.

Please see the item(s) checked below:

✓ You are eligible for benefits until July 31, 2009 and benefits have been cancelled retroactively as of that date.

If you require more information on the status of your premiums, please call RSBC at 1-877-405-4909. If you have questions about your coverage, call Health Insurance BC at one of the numbers below.

Thank you.

Health Insurance BC

C08

Health Insurance BC
www.hibc.gov.bc.ca

PO Box 9035 Stn Prov Govt
Victoria BC V8W 9E3

Lower Mainland: 604 683-7151
Rest of BC: 1 800-663-7100

Did Canadian Prime Minister "Hitler" Harper lie to the Queen of England, Or was that some idiot statement by the Moose Jaw Times Herald in Saskatchewan, Canada?

MOOSE JAW TIMES HERALD MJTIMES.SK.CA

Let's look at this story once again from the Moose Jaw Times Herald:

"Harper meets his Queen in London; he loves her And she loves her favorite Canadian monarchist"
Published on June 13, 2013

Prime Minister Stephen Harper met his Queen in London last night and had tea with her.

Harper, an ardent monarchist, loves the Queen. She loves Harper.

He was supposed to have a 25 minute audience with her, but the 89-year old queen is so fond of Harper that their meeting lasted a full 55 minutes, while other visitors had to cool their heels.

Hopefully Harper told her all the ways he's been promoting the monarchy in Canada, and that's more than merely inviting one set of British royals after another.

The Queen would be pleased to know that Harper has been slapping the word "royal" on everything.

Now we've got the Royal Canadian Navy and the Royal Canadian Air Force.

The Moose Jaw Times Herald
44 Fairford St. W
Moose Jaw, S6H 1V1
Telephone 306-692-6441
Email: editorial@mjtimes.sk.ca

Hmm!

The Queen loves Stephen Harper because Harper has been slapping the word "royal" on everything.

Now we've got the «Royal Canadian Navy" and the «Royal Canadian Air Force. »

Mr.X. saw the Queen of England when she visited Canada in the 1950's:

Dominion anchors Eglinton Town Square. Across Eglinton, Avie Bennett builds the Golden Mile Plaza, a strip with another food store and a cinema. (It is redeveloped 33 years later for the Golden Mile Supercentre). The Township of Scarborough is so enamoured with the cutting-edge Golden Mile Plaza that Queen Elizabeth is brought there in 1959.

During mid 1950s the Golden Mile Plaza was developed just West of the industrial section of the mile, and was visited in 1959 by Queen Elizabeth II, which marked an important part of the community's rich history.

He was a Boy Scout at the time, and his troop was lined up at the Golden Mile Plaza when the Queen's entourage passed by – he remembers the occasion well – he remembers the Queen looking very regal!

He does not remember the Queen looking stupid or gullible?

Maybe, however, Canadian Prime Minister Stephen Harper thinks she is?

Or maybe, Canadian Prime Minister Stephen Harper thinks the Canadian people are?

The point – so Canadian Prime Minister Stephen Harper is telling the Queen of England that he is slapping the word "royal" on everything according to the Moose Jaw Times Herald.

Now we've got the Royal Canadian Navy and the Royal Canadian Air Force.

Hello, hello – that's a crock of "bull shite"!!!

For example, that proud Federal Police Force, The Royal Canadian Mounted Police has been around since 1919:

In 1919, Parliament voted to merge the Force with the Dominion Police, a federal police force with jurisdiction in eastern Canada. When the legislation took effect on February 1, 1920, the name became the Royal Canadian Mounted Police, and headquarters was moved to Ottawa from Regina.

That other Canadian institution the Royal Canadian Navy has been in existence since 1911:

The official title of the navy was the Naval Service of Canada (also Canadian Naval Forces), and the first Director of the Naval Service of Canada was Rear-Admiral Charles Kingsmill (Royal Navy, retired), who had previously been in charge of the Marine Service of the Department of Marine and Fisheries. A request to change name of the Naval Service of Canada to Royal Canadian Navy on 30 January 1911, brought a favourable reply from King George V on 29 August of that year. The naval college was established in the dockyard at Halifax, Nova Scotia in 1911 as "Royal Naval College of Canada".

And now let's look at that other formidable force, the **Royal** Canadian Air Force which was named in 1942:

The history of the Royal Canadian Air Force begins in 1918, when the air force was created as the Canadian Air Force (CAF). In 1924 the CAF was renamed the Royal Canadian Air Force (RCAF) and granted the royal title by King George V.

That idiot Harper wasn't even born until 1959:

Stephen Joseph Harper was born April 30, 1959.

So, exactly what is that "turkey" Stephen Harper telling the Queen – exactly what has he "slapped" the word Royal on???

Is Canadian Prime Minister Stephen Harper "all there"??

He isn't delusional, is he??

Even the mail service in Canada was named in 1867 as *Royal Mail Canada!*

However, it's actually possible idiots like Stephen Harper are trying to re-write Canadian history in their own image!!

As one person wrote:

Is there any source of the Canadian postal service ever being called the "Royal Mail"?

I've looked and I can't find anything.

The photo of the "Royal Mail Canada" mail box seems to bear the royal cypher of King Edward VII.

That's why you get charlatans like Canadian Prime Minister Stephen Harper telling the Queen that he has named the **Royal** Canadian Navy and the **Royal** Canadian Air Force??

Then again, maybe the Moose Jaw Times Herald was writing this story for the "hillbillies" in Saskatchewan who have never heard of the Royal Canadian Navy and the Royal Canadian Air Force before??

And, Mr.X. surely doesn't believe the Queen would have believed that Harper created the names of the Royal Canadian Navy and the Royal Canadian Air Force!!

So who wrote this story for the Moose Jaw Times Herald and what was the purpose??

To make Canadian Prime Minister Stephen Harper look good – it simply has made him out to be a liar or much worse delusional??

Does anyone want to catch Canadian Prime Minister Stephen Harper up on these apparent "lies" to the Queen?

SOME ARTICLES PRIOR TO THE BRITISH COLUMBIA RCMP 1976 & 1979 LIES AND MR.X. 'S SUCCESSFUL SUIT AGAINST THE BRITISH COLUMBIA RCMP!!

Some articles by Mr.X.
former federal peace officer
old age pensioner & PTSD – Chronic Type disability pensioner due to RCMP lies
former Classification Officer BC Maximum Security Penitentiary
former Classification Officer BC Medium Security Mountain Prison
former Probation Officer NFLD Social Services Department*
former Facility Operations Manager Whitbourne Youth Secure Custody

Cognitive development: the functional aspect of symbolization and language,
OCLC Number: 1206866
Publisher: Winnipeg, S. Evans, ©1973.

A bibliography of research on spatial and social behaviour
OCLC Number: 1188853
Publisher: Winnipeg : Thomas Todd Press, 1973.

A bibliography of research on spatial behaviour.
OCLC Number: 123780236
Publisher: Winnipeg : Thomas Todd Press, ©1973.

A note on perceived self-acceptance of institutionalized mentally retarded (IMR) children.
ISSN: 0022-1325
OCLC Number: 105523657
Article
Language: English
Publication: The Journal of genetic psychology, 1973 Sep; 123(1st Half): 171-2
Database: From MEDLINE®/PubMed®, a database of the U.S. National Library of Medicine.

Personal space : direct measurement techniques with hard-of-hearing children
OCLC Number: 8686052
From: Environment and behavior ; v. 6, no. 1 (March 1974).
Publisher: [Beverly Hills, CA] : Sage Publications, 1974.

Effect of discussion on reduction of magnitude of Poggendorff illusion.
ISSN: 0031-5125
OCLC Number: 107527338
Publication: Perceptual and motor skills, 1974 Oct; 39(2): 787-91
Database: From MEDLINE®/PubMed®, a database of the U.S. National Library of Medicine.

Personal space: projective and direct measures with institutionalized mentally retarded children.
ISSN: 0022-3891
OCLC Number: 105929976
Publication: Journal of personality assessment, 1974 Feb; 38(1): 28-31
Database: From MEDLINE®/PubMed®, a database of the U.S. National Library of Medicine.

Personal Space: Projective and Direct Measures with Institutionalized Mentally Retarded Children
ISSN: 0022-3891
OCLC Number: 4631503689
Publication: Journal of Personality Assessment, v38 n1 (19740201): 28-31
Database: ERIC The ERIC database is an initiative of the U.S. Department of Education.

Personal Space: Direct Measurement Techniques with Hard-of-Hearing Children
OCLC Number: 424960945
Accession No: EJ098610
Publication: Environment and Behavior, 6, 1, 117-122, Mar 74
Database: ERIC The ERIC database is an initiative of the U.S. Department of Education.

Personal Space: Direct Measurement Techniques with Hard-of-Hearing Children: Environment and Behavior 6(1) p. 117
N: 0013-9165
OCLC Number: 4647243973
Publication: Environment and Behavior, v6 n1 (19740301): 127-127
Database: ERIC The ERIC database is an initiative of the U.S. Department of Education.

The effect of extended contact with "normals" on the social behavior of hard-of-hearing children.
ISSN: 0022-4545
OCLC Number: 107863896
Publication: The Journal of social psychology, 1975 Feb; 95(First Half): 137-8
Database: From MEDLINE®/PubMed®, a database of the U.S. National Library of Medicine.

The personal space of hard-of-hearing children after extended contact with 'normals'.
ISSN: 0007-1293
OCLC Number: 113775903
Publication: The British journal of social and clinical psychology, 1975 Sep; 14(3): 253-7
Database: From MEDLINE®/PubMed®, a database of the U.S. National Library of Medicine.

The Effect of Extended Contact with "Normals" on the Social Behavior of Hard-of-Hearing Children
OCLC Number: 427052930
Accession No: EJ118344
Publication: Journal of Social Psychology, 95, 137-8, Feb 75
Database: ERIC The ERIC database is an initiative of the U.S. Department of Education.

The personal space of hard-of-hearing children after extended contact with "normals"
OCLC Number: 14151807
Notes: Caption title.
From: British journal of social and clinical psychology ; v. 14, no. 3 (Sept. 1975)
Description: p. 253-257.
Publisher: [Great Britain : s.n., 1975]

The missing person in measurement techniques of interpersonal distance.
OCLC Number: 678920246
Thesis/dissertation : Document : eBook Computer File
Publisher: [Burnaby, B.C.] : [s.n.], ©1975.

The Effect of Extended Contact with "Normals" on the Social Behavior of Hard-of-Hearing Children
ISSN: 0022-4545
OCLC Number: 4653399646
Publication: The Journal of Social Psychology, v95 n1 (19750201): 137-138
Database: ERIC The ERIC database is an initiative of the U.S. Department of Education.

Facilitating the disappearance of perceptual error to the Poggendorff illusion.
ISSN: 0023-8309
OCLC Number: 112913792
Publication: Language and speech, 1976 Apr-Jun; 19(2): 193-9
Database: From MEDLINE®/PubMed®, a database of the U.S. National Library of Medicine.

Incidents of physical assault against child-abuse investigation workers : the nature of child-abuse protection legislation as possible reason for such incidents : some Canadian provincial examples of internal policies attempting to deal with such incidents : placing the trend of such incidents into a theoretical perspective
OCLC Number: 44178037
Thesis/dissertation : Manuscript Archival Material
Publisher: 1994.

Teach your child to read : a simple method for parents and educators
OCLC Number: 61554932 - 1984

The relative effectiveness of whole- and part-task simulators
OCLC Number: 222728551 – 1984

Quality assurance in medical/health care utilizing and incorporating three methods of evaluation: process, setting and outcome : an introduction to assessing medical/health care by means of a conceptual "process matrix" : with special reference to acute care and chronic care hospitals
OCLC Number: 184866019 - 1986.

When the "baby-boom" cohort reaches 65 : will it be social chaos or a carefully planned transition? : an introductory research proposal
OCLC Number: 184861481 - 1986.

Child abuse : a beginning social worker's understanding and use of the DSM-III-R and three reactive mental disorders following child abuse : reactive attachment disorder, post-traumatic stress disorder, and adjustment disorder
Institute of Psychometric Assessment (Bay Roberts, Newfoundland)
OCLC Number: 40533667 - 1994

Dealing with a violent work environment : internal policies and legislation dealing with physical assault and other threats against child protective social workers
Institute of Psychometric Assessment, Applied Studies & Investigative Research.
ISBN: 0969594402 9780969594406
OCLC Number: 35875995 - 1994
Notes: Revision of author's thesis.
Description: vii, 473 leaves; 29 cm.
Series Title: Employee assistance program series.

How to make staff safe: how to reduce labour-management conflict: how to reduce staff grievances
ISBN: 0969594402 9780969594406
OCLC Number: 62920434 - 1997
Other Titles: How to reduce labor-management conflict, How to reduce staff grievances

**Newfoundland - The Lieutenant-Governor in Council may designate probation officers appointed under the Department of Social Services Act to act as probation officers for the purposes of this Act and may designate probation officers appointed under this Act to carry out the duties of probation officers for the purposes of the Department of Social Services Act.*

www.ingramcontent.com/pod-product-compliance
Lightning Source LLC
Chambersburg PA
CBHW081502170526
45166CB00008B/2517
* 9 7 8 1 5 0 0 4 9 1 6 7 3 *